Dearest Jojo,

Enjoy the [...]

long may it [...] .....

THE MINDSET FOR BUSINESS

A definitive GUIDE to getting your mindset in the right
direction to begin and enjoy success in business

Vivienne Joy

Much love always

Vivienne x

10-10-10
Publishing

The Mindset for Business
A definitive GUIDE to getting your mindset in the right direction to
begin and enjoy success in business

Copyright © 2019 Vivienne Joy

ISBN: 9781696536639

Published by:
10-10-10 Publishing
200-455 Apple Creek Blvd.
Markham, Ontario   L3R 9X7

First 10-10-10 Publishing paperback edition October 2019

Table of Contents

Foreword

Do you find that being in business today is tricky? Have you tried, failed, and gone back to a job, and now carry with you the feeling of *not good enough* and not worthy? It doesn't have to be this way.

Pick up this honest, amusing and educational book filled with intelligent questions designed to get you to think differently, act differently, and change some major parts of your life so that you can be successful in business.

The *Ability* chapters take a deeper look at why you are where you are, and how you can change it. You need to know the answer to the question Why? This book will help you understand that for yourself, allowing you to let go of everything that is holding you back.

NLP (neuro linguistic programming) is a huge subject, and a methodology used widely by coaches, therapists and counsellors. This book brings NLP into *your world* in a useful and easy-to-understand way.

Vivienne has not only shared some of her innermost thoughts and experiences, but has kindly gifted you some of her video training modules too. You'll definitely feel differently about being in business when you finish each chapter and do the tasks.

I highly recommend this book!

Raymond Aaron
New York Times Bestselling Author

Acknowledgements

*"Develop an attitude of gratitude, and give thanks for
everything that happens to you, knowing that every step forward
is a step toward achieving something bigger
and better than your current situation."*
– Brian Tracy

Writing a book has been one of my biggest challenges in life (and I've had my fair share!)

The best part was remembering. Remembering some of the amazing people from my past that have shaped my current life and future success. I couldn't possibly mention them all; however, some are featured in this book, so I wanted to give personal thanks.

Pete Allum, the man I prayed for and trusted. My saviour from loneliness. My rock in times of total trauma and desperation, my supportive friend, understanding and trusted partner, for 12 incredible and challenging years of my life. We journeyed and grew together, then apart. I am eternally grateful, and wish you all the love, joy, and luck in the world.

Sharon Oldham, who gave me the inspiration for my first ever business. Without her desire to lose 60 pounds in weight and to convince me to do the Atkins Diet with her, I would never have needed sugar free and low carb chocolate, and discovered that niche.

Janet Knowles, who probably doesn't even remember me but was the professional who introduced me to NLP and the power of the mind. Thank you for showing me how you can be enthusiastic about everything, and approach communication in a different way to the rest of the world to get a different result.

Pam & John Heath, dear departed former bosses and long acquainted friends who believed in me, and backed me emotionally, verbally, and financially with many a business and property venture. Gone but never forgotten.

Lynn Davies, my first real business mentor, who taught me all about profits and sales and recruiting a great team. I do hope you are enjoying your retirement in Portugal.

Adele Doyle, my best friend for many years. We had many good times and tough challenges, and you are now sitting on the sidelines for times of need. There is indeed no friend like an old friend. We know each other inside out, literally.

Becky Adams, a marvellously authentic business genius who helped me understand some basic rules of perception and marketing, and the importance of cake in branding aimed at women. You probably don't know this, but my She-Enjoys coffee, cake, and coaching event name was inspired by you.

Toby & Kate McCartney, my NLP Master Trainers, Supervisors, and role models in the world of personal development. I am grateful to be part of your community and to have received your training to bring forth and update my NLP knowledge and practice. You also gave me the certainty of my public speaking career. Thank you.

Tony Robbins doesn't know me (yet); but he literally changed my world in so many ways when I bought his Get The Edge & Personal Power programme, on tapes via QVC, in 2002. And again, in 2019, when I attended the intensive 4-day 'Unleash The Power Within' event, in London. It was here that I realised my true purpose and legacy; I visioned it, felt it, and am now living it.

Raymond Aaron, my book mentor, author coach, and writing trainer and publisher for sharing wisdom, passion, and past experiences to make sure my book had purpose and was formatted correctly. Also, to his very patient book architects (there were a few) who waited so long for me to get my book done, and never gave up believing it would happen. I'm looking forward to publishing many more with your support and guidance in the future, to enable prospective business owners to get the help they need for many years to come.

To the coaches, trainers, mentors, guides, clients, partners, friends, competitors, copycats, allies, peers, and influencers... Your words, actions, intentions, inspiration, education, motivation, methods, and teachings travel my journey with me to this day and always, including: Elaine McBride, Taz Thornton, Asha Clearwater, DK Green, Julie Foster, Lenka Lutonska, Shaa Wasmund, Nigel Botterill, Andy Gibney, Nicki Vee, Nick James, Kerrie Rycroft, my original *She-Thrives Tribe* (Yasmin Ali, Judith Hanson, Tracey Robertson, Georgina Hodgkinson, Lindsey Marriott, Jane McCourt, Susan Royle, Jojo Bailey, Caroline Prout, Helen Buckley, Sonya Kolodziejska, and Debbie Bunce), Jo Blackwell, Marie-Louise O'Neill, Sam Adams, Julie Valentine, Yvonne Michele, Greg Poole, Debbie Kirton, Jodie Groves, Ebony Staite, Mark Brereton, and many more.

And of course, my biggest gratitude belongs with my always loved and missed Mum & Dad (Hedy & Ken). You lived a tough life and did your best to give me all I have by way of confidence, self-belief, determination, and joy. Joy by name and by nature.

Introduction

"You never know when a moment
and a few sincere words can have an impact on a life."
~ Zig Ziglar

This book was promised...

I was asking some basic questions about *business foundations* to a perplexed looking, desperately confused and overwhelmed, newish (2 years or so) business owner. She was trying her absolute best to stand out in a LOUD, heavily populated online market, and earn a basic living. It was clear that she was scared to do anything differently from her competition, didn't know how to be more visible to prospects, didn't know how to position herself to prove her credibility, and had no sales process or marketing plan to speak of. In fact, sales were the last priority on her list, and she was confused about social platforms and websites... Add to that a load of guilt around not spending enough time with her partner and family, or contributing enough to the family income pot!

GUILT and FEAR were sitting heavily in her heart and mind, and affecting her negatively! She was stuck and didn't know how to even start to shift and improve. *"Thank fuck I found you at that business networking event!"* Her words, not mine, but I absolutely agreed! She was still very much in start-up mode, and needed a plan that felt right. Let's be clear here; I'm not talking about the kind of business plan you take to the Bank Manager, or create using a template from the internet, or make with a non-mindset-shifting Business Coach who focuses mainly on the numbers and activity, and not on the person behind them... I mean, she wasn't even clear on the what, where, when, how much, and who that this business was created for. She was lost and confused. Then came a rather awkward conversation about profits, turnover, costs, prices, and direction, where I felt like I was some business reality TV show investor!

I felt for her, truly I did—for her and ALL the business owners suffering from *imposter syndrome*, feeling not good enough, not worthy, and stuck. *I remember it well.*

I remember first feeling it 25 years ago in a senior management position. I landed a great job and salary, but looking back, I didn't have the experience, confidence, or skills to succeed, and NO TRAINING was on offer to fill this gap. I was winging it. It was painful and damaging, and I believed I was crap at the job. It took me a lot of deep mindset work to shift just this one experience, let alone all the other career challenges!

Have you been there in some part of your life? Maybe you're there now. I called it "out of my depth," and I was swimming for dear life, my head just above the water, breathless, anxious, and exhausted. I couldn't see a safe haven, or a place to rest until the waters were calm. This story doesn't end well. I remember bursting into tears one day in the boardroom, when I was asked a TRIGGER question... Brian bellowed, "Do you have any idea what you are going to do to sell all of this excess stock, Vivienne? It owes us fifty thousand pounds." I looked at him like a rabbit in the headlights. It was a trigger question, because I didn't have a clue. I had forecasted sales of these products based on what I wanted to achieve, and not on the reality of a new skincare range in the UK. They had purchased product to my sales forecast, and it was all sitting in a warehouse going out of date!

I could feel my face going red and tears stinging the corners of my eyes. As I trembled anxiously, I couldn't stop the drops from falling. The more I panicked, the drier my mouth got, and the less likely I was to find a logical answer for Brian. It was a terrifying moment. In this moment, I could feel my budding career going down the toilet, my parents' disappointment in their only superstar daughter, my boyfriend telling me to get a more local job so he could see more of me, and the fear of not being able to pay the mortgage!

Did my mind have a diva-exaggerated panic? Yes, it absolutely did. I created a strong belief in that moment that I was rubbish at business. You can see how I came to that conclusion from this one lacking skillset. I was from a service-based industry, and products were rather new.

I'm sure you can identify with this form of catastrophising from events in your own life, it's based on nothing but blind FEAR and debilitating self-talk, which puts the body into fight, flight, or freeze mode. *I froze.*

In this time of FEAR, I had two choices:

Face Everything And Rise
Fear Everything And Resign!

I left the office in a desperate state, and I sobbed and sobbed. As someone who doesn't consider failure as an option, I sat in my beloved company car, in the car park, until there were no more tears. I wiped my blotchy face, drank the McDonald's coffee, smoked the fifth cigarette (yuk, can't believe I did that for 16 years of my life), and thought, *"Fuck You Brian; I'll show you."*

And so, **Vivienne the Brave** was born in business... *And show him, I did.*

So, back to my client-coaching story: This amazingly talented and genuinely nice woman was sitting in front of me, shuffling uncomfortably as she started to understand why her business wasn't making the impact and money that she had dreamed of. You see, she was bloody brilliant at her craft; she just hadn't had the training to get the skills, knowledge, or experience in critical areas of her business—*mindset, sales, marketing, and strategy.*

She looked me in the eye and said, with such meaning, "If only there was a book with all of this mindset for business stuff, I wouldn't have wasted the last year feeling like a failure! You should write one, Vivienne. Please write one, for me!"

I felt her plea, and I gulped as I realised that all business owners need *owner-managed* business skills training, and I was just the person to provide it. Not because I'm a superstar famous person or millionaire—actually, it's exactly for that reason. *Because if a normal working-class woman can create six-figure businesses and beyond, you can too!*

That night, as I watched TV, her words, *"Please write one for me,"* rang through my ears, and I felt it deep in my soul. I grabbed a pen and notepad, and started to write this book. As I wrote the *Ability* chapters of the book, I also wrote a training programme, which is enjoyed by many today. I have been writing training and coaching programmes to help as many people as I can, ever since... It did, however, take me THREE years to *finish* this book. A fair scattering of procrastination—*I'm too busy*, perfectionism, and *I'm not good enough* bullshit—got in the way! Also, once I started writing, I couldn't stop, and in fact, wrote 4 books at the same time! There's a lot to share—too much in fact; business challenges and solutions are ever evolving.

It wasn't easy to decide what to put in this book. In fact, it has been quite a painful journey for me. I had to get out of my own way too! "Why me? Why should I write a book? Who would buy it?"... Blah blah, scared, blah blah, how will I, blah blah blah... Oh, do shut up,

Vivienne's inner child saboteur. You won't win; she just **promised** her client, and she never, ever breaks a client promise—*not ever*!

Mindset, sales, marketing, and strategy are the essential foundations, and we are going to work through them together in these chapters. *I am overjoyed to share my experiences, skills, and knowledge with you. Let's do this!*

About the Author and Book

*"One who has been where you are
and has made it to my dream life."*
~ Vivienne Joy

I still occasionally revisit where you are now, but I'm armed with the mindset and tools to get unstuck and even laugh at myself... I'm going to teach you how to do this too! **You CAN** enjoy the journey to business success.

Having coached, trained, mentored, advised, and lovingly prodded many business owners out of their own way, I realised we are all the same. Start-up, stuck, failing, or expanding business owners—*the problems are all basically caused by the same three things for us all!*

Mindset. Mind set in the wrong direction. Busy focusing on fears and problems, and not on solutions and successes. *Sounds simple, doesn't it.* It is when you have the right tools and if you even notice that you're stuck in the wrong cycle.

Skills. No real experience or skills in starting, managing, selling, marketing, and expanding a business. A case of, *you don't know what you don't know, and are simply trying to do your best.* It's a bit like building a house and not knowing how to set the foundations, lay the bricks, or ensure that the roof is supported with a sound structure. It will simply not last.

Strategy. If you don't know where you are going, or why, are you likely to get there? *Who knows!* You wouldn't start your car and just drive without knowing your destination. Eventually, you'd be lost, frustrated, and out of energy or gas—*sound familiar?*

Successful business owners have changed their mindset for business to match their new destination. They've faced their fears, changed their self-beliefs and money beliefs, and have upskilled to create a strategy that they follow consistently, joyfully, and seemingly (annoyingly) effortlessly, until they get to their destination. They then choose another goal, and *rinse and repeat!*

Where are you in this cycle? Would you like to know how you've ended up where you are now?

The mind gets stuck in the past—a bit like a broken record. Thoughts are created with a **rule book of old beliefs** formed by the *child version of you,* who has learned from people around them, who they trusted to know better during the formative years (think parents and teachers), or by personal experiences and comparison to others (good and bad).

Basically, this child version of you is probably running parts of your business (and life) right now!

That *little you* is a scared one who lacks confidence—one that doesn't want to stand out, and one who doesn't believe they are special and can be an overachiever—and that little (or big) voice in your head stops you from getting on with shit, and makes you avoid the real stuff that will make a difference to your business, your income, your joy, and your life! The *little you* needs to play and be naughty, or hide and keep safe. The *adult you* wants and needs business success, to make a difference and to achieve life security.

Who wins?

The challenges, fears, doubts, sabotaging self-talk, avoidance behaviours, and lack of knowledge that you experience are VERY common. That's right; all the things you feel are NORMAL and can be changed with the right training, coaching, mentoring, and mindset. I'm hoping that this is good news for you!

Right now, you possibly feel like there's a lot of work to do... and that may well be the case. We will get it all sorted for you, I promise. I'm going to teach you all sorts of NLP-based techniques, coaching tools, mindset mastery, business skills, and much, much more throughout these pages... It is my mission to help you think, feel, behave, and achieve in a way more suited to the life you want.

Let's Be Honest...

How is business going? Maybe you haven't started yet and are still braving the day job.

I'm not suggesting that YOU are suffering from imposter syndrome, or don't have the basics in place; but I'm figuring that something is clearly not going so well for you in your career, or you'd be doing something different with your time right now other than reading this book.

So, just to be sure, I'm going to cover all the basics to make sure you create a profitable and joyful business from this moment forward. It's worth having a **read of all the chapters**; you know, just to make sure that you have all bases covered—and I repeat, do use the FREE Academy video training modules, where you will get to meet me personally. I hope to meet you, too, one day! :)

The lovely client who provided me my own eye opening, *oh shit*, shift moment, wasn't alone. We are all the same! We are all second-guessing our choices, doing our best, realising where we are going wrong, and sabotaging and beating ourselves up, whilst putting on a brave face to friends, family, clients, and peers: "I'm great; business is going well."

NOW is when that "brave face" stops my friend. We are going to get you sorted so that when you say those words, you actually mean them! Sound good?

Business is a HUGE subject, and I'm sure you know that there are a million trillion coaches, books, and videos out there. Thank you for choosing to trust me and my words, experiences, and beliefs to transform your own!

This book is what I consider to be THE DEFINITIVE BASICS that I use with my business empowerment clients.

After lots of typing and deleting on my now knackered laptop, I eventually had to decide that good enough is good enough: A non-perfect book, read by many, is worth more in the world than a perfect one that never left my laptop!

I recorded your **FREE bonus videos** because some people learn better by watching and listening than they do by reading text. As an outcome-focused coach, my main goal is that you get what you need to get unstuck and enjoy success! I also figured that if you see my happy, helpful face, you might decide that you want more of my no-nonsense style and obvious experience of super success, fucking failure, and a whole load of stuff in between, and want me as your personal coach.

To get your FREE videos, go to www.MindsetForBusiness.co.uk/BookDownloads, and enter your email address, and you will be directed to the *Mindset for Business Academy*, for your freebies.

You'll soon work out that I am blatantly, transparently honest (probably too honest). So, on the link you visit, you can also see more of what I do. Whilst I still have breath in my lungs and a sound mind, I will be constantly creating more affordable tools and training to keep you going for many years of business transformation success... I hope you enjoy :)

If I've done my job correctly, and you actually do the MINDSHIFT Tasks in each chapter (I know, I've skipped them too in other books), you will get plenty of "oh shit, that is so obvious" shifts throughout these easy-to-read ability bursts. You'll start to think and behave differently as you learn the ability and enjoy your life and business.

If you are not enjoying your life, what is the fucking point!?

Why me?

"Why me?" I heard myself say... "Why not me?" I heard myself answer. So here we are.

I consider myself to be lucky, talented, and resourceful.
(Positive mindset belief right there—we keep the positive ones.)

The truth is, the harder I work and the smarter I get with personal development and getting myself out there, the luckier I appear to get—funny that! Someone once said to me, "Darling, I don't need luck; luck is for losers, and I'm a winner!" *Loved that attitude.*

Any Coach, Consultant, Expert or Guru that tells you that success is effortless, and that money just floats in whilst sleeping, is selling you a beautiful picture of a journey that you would like to have, rather than the level of work that is truly needed. *A bit like the equivalent of a quick fix diet.*

I see conferences filled with wide-eyed, aspiring entrepreneurs, listening avidly to skilled sales people, on stages, selling the next *quick business fix or hack.* The long and short of it is that you will only get out, in the long term, what you put in NOW. I'll say that again. If you build it properly, with passion, and invest in yourself and your systems, your business WILL pay off with rewards and euphoria beyond your wildest dreams... this *rarely* happens overnight. Behind every *overnight success* is someone who has been slogging away, investing and strategically building their brand and offerings. You just see the *tipping point results,* and want to get to that as quickly as you believe they did!

I was the same. I thought it looked easy... I had LOADS of business skills gained through managing, saving, and growing other people's business empires, yet with my current business, I still had to learn the hard way, and it is my mission that you *earn whilst you learn,* and enjoy the journey!

Now, you might not be remotely interested in my CV, career, or business journey; in which case, you can skip to the first Ability chapter. However, the lessons I've learned have been SO critical to the belief map I created, I felt it my duty to share them to let you *consider your own,* and also to show you precisely why I am qualified by experience (as well as by certificates) to help you on your business journey.

Your past career equals your beliefs now.

Go and find some clues for yourself of why you feel and behave how you do. *There may also be your first few tasks in there—enjoy!*

The Real CV/Resumé

Most of us spend our days trying to be the person we want to be—or think we should be!

We want to fit in and be accepted, whilst also standing out and being recognised. *Can you already start to see where your struggle is—that you can't do both?*

Nothing demonstrates our ability to present THE BEST VERSION of us in our glory than the often *rather fabricated* CV/resume. One of my friends even has *made up jobs and dates* on hers, as she simply can't remember them all. This never stopped her from being the Commercial Director of a rather large corporate… *That secret is safe with me. The reason I know is that I wrote her CV! I've always been OK at creative writing :)*

How creative is your CV—especially the hobbies and achievements bit? I hate exercise, yet mine has a pretty list that makes me look NOT lazy!

Just to be clear, I'm not looking for a job, although it's flattering that I get asked so often. I'm totally unable to have a boss ever again. I am most definitely the boss in my life! I do, however, still happily do regular consultancy for organisations that I'm interested in, or that have real challenges, so definitely ask if you want my help.

If my REAL CV (written in the third person for some random reason as they always are) was REALLY honest, it would read like this…

PERSONAL STATEMENT

Lucky, working class, not degree educated, and lazy Vivienne Joy Cox, landed fabulous job after fabulous job, gave it her all, tried to impress and fit in, and still ended up broke and rejected.

Please give her a job so she can pay the mortgage, make her parents proud, and remind herself that she has any real worth in the world, before she eats and drinks herself to an early death, whilst watching repeats of the sitcom, "Friends."

(Note: Redundant is the business version of rejected. I was made redundant 3 times—joyful, not!)

Listen to my **identity tags** created by my story (we call them beliefs), and they rule everything.

TASK:
I wonder what your career beliefs truly are. What would your CV overview REALLY read?

Write a sentence with *4 belief words* and *an outcome* that describes your career (like I have above). This is who you believe you have been/or still are.

EDUCATION

SCHOOL: Couldn't wait to leave HER third senior school, aged 16, as was bullied at the second one and hated every minute of the boring classes, fake friends, games lessons, and the uniform that she refused to wear. The only part she liked was the safety and certainty of school dinners, flirting with boys, and *double art* with Miss Roscoe.

QUALIFICATIONS: By some miracle, as she did no revision, Vivienne achieved 9 GCSEs, and an ability to touch type and talk a lot and influence people by sharing every thought that comes into her head (*which got me into trouble daily*).

Real School Report: "If only Vivienne could stop talking long enough to study, she would be a scholar!"

COLLEGE: Went to Tresham Secretarial College, in Kettering, Northants, for 3 months. Only did this as the school career advisor told her to, and she couldn't work out what having an A-level art would give her as a career. Going to college was the only time she's ever done as she was told—*and the advisor was wrong!* Learnt to eat a huge lunch in the cheap café, and to fall asleep, in the afternoons, from pure boredom in Teeline shorthand classes.

JOBS

Volvo Trucks – Sales Ledger Clerk 1988 (jeez, she feels old; the good old 80s – learnt accounts and passed driving test first time; very chuffed with herself)

A girl named Tracey, who she went to secondary school and secretarial college with, got a job as a secretary, and said there was one available. Viv got on 2 buses—in her tights, stilettos, and pencil skirt—and flirted through the interview. Colin, the Office Manager, took a shine to her cocky *"Of course, I can do that"* attitude and chattiness, and gave her the job on the spot *(Belief was born: "I get every job I apply for.")*. When she got home to tell her excited parents, she hadn't a clue what she had accepted, apart from the hours and the pay, £4,800 per annum (bless her, eh). *(Belief and work ethic born: Earn money and make parents proud.)*

After about 4 years at Volvo, she was bored and believed she could've literally run the whole accounts department, which on reflection, probably wasn't true; but she was told by her mum that she was amazing, and why would her mum lie! *(Belief: "I can do anything if I put my mind to it," and, "I must keep learning new things to stop the boredom.")*

One day, she called a man to chase money owing, and he asked if she was in sales. He said that she had too much personality to be sitting on a phone all day, and that she should go into sales and make loads of money! *(Belief was born: Use personality to make money.)* She thanks Paul from Paul's Transport: I owe you one!

American Express – Financial Planner 1992 (the 90s were so much fun, and there was a lot of hairspray – learnt sales). After Paul suggesting sales, she bought the local jobs paper that night and saw a vacancy that appeared to describe her. She called the advert, and spoke to a very smooth and charming man called David. She went for the interview one evening, and got the job immediately (obviously deepening the belief around always getting every job).

There was a problem. She was only 20, and legally couldn't start the *commission only* job for 4 months. So, for that whole time, she went from her day job to her new job (FOR FREE), and learnt telesales. She loved it; it was a different world of freedom. The people there were all swanky grownups, and treated her like one too. They earned lots of money and worked VERY hard. *(Belief: Hard work equals hard-earned cash.)*

Shortly after her 21st birthday, she qualified with a financial planning certificate after 2 exciting weeks of residential training in Slough, Berkshire, on building rapport and personality profiling, which she absolutely loved from the first word. She'd never stayed in a hotel before, and she met Dean, who looked like Patrick Swayze, and she, ahem, revised with him most nights! It was her first taste of *executive lifestyle,* with a paid-for, 3-course dinner, wine, and full English—she had found her home.

Sadly, the job, and the Swayze lookalike guy, lasted for 4 months before she had enough of working in the evenings, and she signed on with a recruitment agency... She had also naively chosen the wrong market to sell life insurance, etc., and struggled. VERY important business lesson right there! *(New painful belief: Choose a market you know and love, and give them what they need!)*

Recruitment Agency – (learnt business launch, management, and expansion) – The primary Consultant interviewed her, then another did, and another, then the MD. Four hours later, a rather confused Viv had a job at the recruitment agency as a consultant. She also had her first parking ticket, in the Northampton multi-storey car park, for £25!

Spent a year selling and negotiating, and was moved to start up a totally new branch in her home town of Kettering, Northants, with her own team (aged 21). She trusted her Secretary (another Tracey) way too much, and treated her like a friend. Tracey totally shafted her! Told a pack of lies, got Viv fired, and took the Branch Manager job for herself! It hit Viv hard, but she didn't go down for long. Her self-talk was, "Their loss; I'll show them," and she did. *(Belief: Be careful whom you trust; there is no such thing as a friend at work.)*

Design Agency – (learnt marketing and branding) – She was thrilled to get the first job she applied for: Account Executive, selling talented London Designers' expertise to leading brands all over the UK.

She felt very successful rocking up to Virgin Interactive to take design briefs for their latest release computer game packaging. She got a taste of London and liked it—hardly surprising, as she was born there, and both her parents were too! She fit drinks in after work, and even loved the daily train commute, and her MASSIVE mobile phone!

Global Advertising Agency – (learnt business, profits, and strategy) – It didn't take career-driven Vivienne long to *outgrow* the design agency—about a year, in fact. She wanted to earn more and achieve more. She picked up the trusty newspaper and sent her CV to MKH. She met Lynn in the pub for an informal interview. She was a gregarious character who was starting a satellite office for a bigger organisation, and she had a good pedigree as a Director of a huge group of newspapers. She really knew her stuff, and it shone brightly. Vivienne believed in Lynn, and Lynn believed in Vivienne.

She was employed on £15,000 per annum, to business generate through cold calling, to sell recruitment advertising services to local companies needing to advertise in newspapers all over the world. Working from the annex at her boss's house, it all happened very quickly. The business grew in turnover, profit, and team members. Viv learnt a lot, managed staff, and launched new niche divisions of the agency, which in year 2 was in huge offices in Central Northampton. During her 4 years there, Vivienne personally created a £1 million business, was earning pretty good money, and was having great fun with colleagues (vodka shots instead of dinner, and no sleep Thursdays!). The wipe clean white boards became everything: figures, targets, and bonuses!

Let's take a CV break for a paragraph; some important stuff happened here...

The first big turning point in my career life was at age 24. I was introduced to the world of NLP, by a Sales rainer named Janet. The all-female team of the advertising agency, in Northampton, England, had been gifted this training to help us reach our ever-increasing divisional sales targets. I think we saw it as a bit of a work skive with a long yummy lunch, so we were well up for it! Janet arrived, and we sat in astonishment at her enthusiasm for EVERYTHING—it was like she spoke in another language—and we were mesmerised.

We started off by moaning about our jobs, our boss, our clients, our pay, our commissions, the hours... oh, and anything else we could moan about—poor us, eh? Within hours, we were as enthusiastic as her. We stopped moaning, and started seriously achieving and thriving. The lessons and techniques I learnt from Janet about rapport building, persuasive communications, and business are still a relevant part of my life and what I teach now. NLP is a life tool that will change everything for you. It's why I am now a fully certified NLP Trainer, NLP Master Practitioner, NLP Hypnotherapist, and NLP Master Coach... I live it, eat it, and breathe it, and along with a huge toolkit of other techniques and methodology, it is how I change lives and businesses today. It's also what I will be teaching you throughout this book. If you ever read this, *Janet Knowles*, thank you for giving me such a good start in NLP; and thank you to the now-retired-to-Portugal, *Lynn Davies,* for teaching me the nuts and bolts of business, and for bringing Janet to your team. *Very grateful indeed.*

I got a bit tearful typing that; writing a book is rather emotionally fascinating—like a massive trip down memory lane!

Ahem, anyway, back to the CV...

Leading Hair & Beauty Wholesaler – After NLP, Vivienne learnt to grab opportunities and make opportunities! One of her clients made an offer she couldn't refuse: to switch from agency side to client side (from selling to buying), with a great bonus, company car, and European travel 6 times a year. Yep, she went for it quicker than they could write the Senior Manager offer letter!

She learnt troubleshooting, product launches, and BIG business challenges (like Brian!), reporting to the board and being responsible for large quantities of stock and budgets. She sourced and launched European brands into the UK, and learned the value of channel to market and cross selling.

She wrote and designed their first ever website, when companies didn't really have websites as they were so new (it was that long ago), and was parachuted into other parts of the business... The training academy that wasn't making profit, she turned that around and managed a nationwide sales team of Beauty Therapists that didn't believe they could sell (enter training skills sharpening!). Visited large salons and spas, selling high-end launch packages, and helping them to increase their client spend and sales in their business, whilst training their staff too! Vivienne bloody loved this. Her knowledge and skills impacted the salon owners and teams immediately and dramatically. *(Powerful Belief: People listen to you and take action; you change lives, and it feels amazing.)*

Vivienne loved this job. Sadly, life had other ideas for her.

CV ends. Life ends...

It was all going ridiculously well. I felt like an integral part of the organisation, and became a personal friend to the millionaire owners. Then my life changed dramatically—a year that truly turned me upside down and inside out, and basically made life unliveable—Vivienne Joy Cox's "oh, fuck" year. Some coaches call it the breakdown to the breakthrough. I look back and thank the Universe for the people and skills that supported me through the most tragic of times.

Just after my 29th birthday, in 2001, my mum, aged 66, was diagnosed with cancer (for the second time), and this time, it was terminal. As an only child, I was devastated, and I was worried about my 73-year-old dad and how he would cope—he was still working full time to make ends meet, and *my parents lived with me*. The impact of Mum about to die at any point was catastrophic.

My bosses of 4 years, Pam and John Heath, were amazing (and have sadly left this world now too). They allowed me to work as I could, knowing I would get the work done through the night if I had to. My dear old dad and I nursed Mum for a year until she passed. It was the toughest and most rewarding time of my life. We were lucky to have a year, as she had been given just weeks at diagnosis. *(Positive Belief: Be there for people, and you will be valued.) (Negative belief: Nothing is forever, no matter how much you want it.)*

My mum was my everything, and it was hard—very hard—harder than my unconscious allows me to remember 17 years on. I returned to work and life (just about), going through the motions. If you have lost the person you love most in the world, I know that you'll get what I mean. I was numb but was doing my best.

Then, 8 months later, my dad had a massive heart attack in Spain, and he died too. It floored me. I was with him at the time, through a catastrophe of medical errors. (That's another story for another book. I literally couldn't have made it all up.) My best friend of 10 years moved 2 hours away, and I truly felt alone for the first time in my life.

I felt alone because I was alone.

Learn to accept change...

2002/2003 saw me lose everything I knew and loved, even my mum's dearest sister. That life breakdown that coaches talk about; this was mine, and I couldn't do a fucking thing to change what had happened. I couldn't control or manage the change. I had to just allow it.

My career was the last thing on my mind. I felt like a victim of fate, spiralling into a "fuck it" pattern of chain smoking, gambling, addictive eating, habitual shopping, drugs, clubbing, and all-night binge drinking in an attempt to simply numb the pain and escape my harsh reality. My self-talk was often, "Why me? Poor me." Nothing positive was ever going to come from any of that behaviour, and I didn't even realise I was so low.

Thankfully, and luckily (still lucky amongst the tragedy as it's a core belief), I had just met THE man; the one that was to later be my husband. He was a rock of a man, with high emotional intelligence and a huge love and care for me. I thank the Universe daily still for sending me an earth saviour. Pete Allum wasn't perfect (although I called him Perfect Pete); he had his own challenges, but we fell in love. We saved each other, for which I will always be eternally grateful. *(Belief: Be grateful for all the help you receive; the Universe really has got your back, even when you don't think it has—believe.)*

I started to care about life again...

My Mum's words, *"Start your own business; you'll never be rich while you work for someone else!"* rang in my ears often (thanks for that belief Mum). I'm sure she was and still is my muse! For a 5ft-nothing woman, she had almighty strength and persuasion. *I got that from her!*

She tried to get my dad to have a business once; but he was a builder and really didn't have the business skills, and he made himself ill! Luckily, I was only eight at the time and didn't realise what had happened to him, or I might have created a belief around business being bad for you! *(See how easily these beliefs are created!)*

With my wayward partying, *coping* lifestyle, I'd gained a fair amount of weight, and my friend and former work colleague, Sharon Oldham, started following the Atkins diet, which was all the rage in 2003. Sharon and I were doing well on the plan, but we REALLY missed chocolate and cake! We found a USA website that was selling sugar free and low carb versions... Excitedly, we ordered our goodies, ignoring the ridiculous pricing. *(Belief: People will pay anything for what they truly want and need.)*

A sweet business...

It was a month from ordering to delivery, and nearly £100 in delivery fees! I saw a huge gap in the market for sugar deprived, chocolate loving dieters who would pay anything for a treat... I was right, and I was serving a market that I knew well—it was me. *(Belief: Find a commercial gap, and serve it what it wants and needs.)* I got in touch with manufacturers, and asked to be a UK distributor. My niche retail business was born, grew quickly, and flourished—I TOTALLY threw myself into it, working 18-hour days sometimes! *I swapped coping strategies for success strategies.*

I re-mortgaged my house to invest, and invest and invest a bit more, in marketing. I tried loads of techniques, had training, and developed myself and my mindset! *I was a worthy investment...*

Although I'd lived NLP since the earlier days, NLP came back into my life at this point, like a long-lost saviour. My best friend, Adele, didn't want to take the course on her own. It was free, so I agreed to accompany her. Thanks, Adele Doyle; you helped me get out of my own way, and changed my life for the better that day!

I called it the **Sugar Free Superstore,** as I wanted to look like a huge organisation, and I knew I could do whatever I liked! I turned over 6 figures in my first year, from my house! There was chocolate piled high in every room. Pete put our bed into the lounge. It was insane and fun, and I adored my business. It literally saved me from the hedonistic distraction I had been using to try to recover.

Every year was good, until year 4. Nestle made a low carb KitKat, and low carb became mainstream in the UK. My competitors became HUGE supermarkets, with HUGE buying power, and I couldn't compete without becoming a manufacturer of food—not something I wanted to do, so I got out. I sold the domain and business structure to my nearest competitor, which was great experience. *(Belief: I'm not as big as the big players.)*

After I sold my business, my husband and I built a house, and I didn't really know what else to do. I wasn't keen on the idea of getting a job. Having written £20,000 stock cheques, the salaries on offer looked ridiculously low, and the jobs looked boring compared to the excitement of doing it my way!

TASK:

Your money mindset standard's *norms* are powerful… What are yours?

What is a low salary/income to you (your floor)?

What is an unachievably high salary/income to you (your ceiling)? I bet you don't pay yourself your floor every month in your business, do you?)

So, what is REALLY your financial floor?

Being an employee (again)

A few months of being a lady of leisure, with plenty of holidays, a Porsche, a speedboat, and a 19-foot camper, and now 2 houses, I was pondering my purpose (as you do!) and asking the Universe for some signs or direction of what to do next.

I was out for a Friday wine bar session with a close friend, Jo... She mentioned tentatively that she *needed a favour* to help out a tricky situation at the Global Recruitment Agency that she managed. As I sipped wine, laughed, and enjoyed the English setting sun in the beer garden, it seemed like a perfectly fab and fun idea to help her out for 12 weeks as her Recruitment Consultant, on £17k a year. I knew the job backwards from years ago, and figured it was *a good place to find a better job*—it was; and I did. I was back on the career path and skipping along! *(Belief: When you don't NEED the money, life is a fun game!)*

One day, a leading adhesive manufacturer needed a General Manager to get them out of financial trouble. They were in a huge mess in every area of the business. The UK was just going in to *double dip recession* 2007, and the USA polymer market was negatively impacting their UK companies. I simply went to take the job brief to help them recruit... and lucky me, got offered the job on the spot, by the feisty Irish owner.

He had his own ideas and rules, and so did I.

It was the least *politically correct* interview I had ever witnessed (still to this day)! He asked me if I wanted to have kids (not his, although it wouldn't have surprised me), told me I was too old to do so anyway, and that chances were slim at my weight! The HR Manager was in bits, and was ashen and anxious. I thought it was hilarious! At the end, he looked me straight in the eye and said (in a broad Irish accent), "Are you going to come and sort my fucking company out?" to which I replied, "Depends on how much you're going to fucking pay me!" I'm pretty sure my response got me a £7k car allowance, a huge office, a team of 50, and a salary I had never earned before (even in my business).

My demand of him was that he left me to get on with it. I would run it like it was my own company, and report monthly. He wasn't to question anything—which to my amazement, he did! *(Belief: Fortune favours the brave.)*

After a year, I had turned the business around, relaunched their master £4 million brand, and basically—wait for it— made my role redundant! This was very convenient for the job-stealing bitch from another part of the business, who took over the role for a lot less money. *(Belief: Success brings enemies and pain.)*

This hit me hard. I had never been rejected (made redundant) before.

The big realisation was that *positive thinking* is easy when life is good.

It's a REAL challenge when you lose your confidence and drive. I had to dig deep. Very deep. I learnt a lot about myself and my self-talk at this time… I would wake up and say to myself, "Another thankless day of job hunting," as I lay in bed not wanting to get up. I QUICKLY learnt to reframe it to, "I wonder which amazing opportunities I'll uncover today." It's easier to get up in the morning with that self-talk, eh!

TASK:

What is your *first thing in the morning* self-talk—does it enable or disable you?

Write all your morning thoughts down. Identify which ones empower you, and keep them.

Those that don't, reframe them, just as I did above!

I returned to recruitment for a while, working part time with a local HR organisation who wanted to add another channel to their business to help clients recruit. I made myself redundant there, too, once the division was created, so I went and did it for myself with the help of my former bosses, Pam and John, who invested in me. *(Belief: I am worth it.)*

The birth of business number two, in 2011, **Vivico Recruitment Ltd** (remember, my maiden name was **Vivi**enne **Cox**), was joyous, and I did six figures in my first year (again), and every year. *(Belief: I will always turn over at least 6 figures every year in business.)* I built a team, had lovely offices, and started business networking and building a name for myself. I learnt so much. In year 2, I nearly lost the business, as I overtraded, and I took on too many service staff and not enough sales staff. I also learnt not to work with family or friends. My husband, joining the business, saw the demise of our marriage (amongst other reasons), *but that's for another book, believe me!*

I finally found my thing

In 2013, I finished my NLP training journey, qualifying as an NLP Trainer and MasterCoach. I was already mentoring and advising businesses around their people strategies and business processes, so it seemed to make sense to coach and train further, to really provide a fully rounded business success solution—*which I LOVE!*

The recruitment business eventually evolved and became part of my group brand structure today, supporting businesses to shift and scale. I hold Speaker Summits, provide online coaching and training, one-to-one transformation, coaching cards, and the Academy that you will be enjoying. I work with start-up businesses, right through to global enterprises that are evolving; with the MD, Directors, management teams, sales teams, and customer services, to help join up their communications, get them speaking the same language to each other, and the right language to themselves, to get the very best results. I love it, at all levels; it's about helping people to empower themselves to transform and evolve... Watching business owners *get out of their own way* is my new addiction—it's better than all the drugs, shopping, gambling, and drinking! The significance I make to the lives of others gives me a buzz every time, and makes me *know my worth* in the world—it's what they call *"living your purpose."*

Today, I lead a laptop lifestyle (not the photographed Ferrari type, but in real life). I am typing this final paragraph, overlooking the pool from my friend's stunning villa in the South of France. I have created a business that I can blissfully enjoy on my own terms, and from anywhere in the world, and it changes the world for people every day.

Today, I am proud of myself. I just said that out loud!

TASK:

How often are you proud of yourself?

List all the times you've been proud of yourself in career and business.

Now that you have done this task, you can say it out loud too.

Read out loud all the things you are proud of yourself for. State it, stand up, and shout it: "I am proud of myself because of...."

Given my original life and beliefs at the beginning of the book, I have come a long way, eh?

Was it easy? No. Was it quick? No... Was it worth it? *Fuck, Yes.*

It may sound pretentious and smug, but I have worked hard, worked clever, and worked consistently (even when I didn't feel like it) to get my dream. I love my life every day. If you had told me that this journey would have taken me here, and that it would feel so joyful, I would never have believed it.

I now have a new dream that is fast becoming a mission. I'm sure you'll hear all about it soon…

My legacy and purpose, the **She-Enjoys Life Foundation (SELF), is** helping charity owning women all over the world to change the world—a true business movement of talented, supportive, and determined women, wanting to make a significant contribution and serve their purpose. *Get involved and help us, at www.She-EnjoysLife.com.*

I'm here to tell you and show you living proof… Your life and business CAN be (and WILL be) different for you too, if you follow the 7 rules of life success…

1. Do the work on your mindset. *Daily. Always.*

2. Get the sales, marketing, management, and strategy skills. *Business mastery, check out my boot camp.*

3. Have a plan that you truly connect with and can vision for yourself. *Vision it daily, like it is real.*

4. Learn to trust and believe in yourself. *And tell yourself daily.*

5. Be proud of yourself along the way. It is a powerful emotion; it helps wipe away tears, and years of shitty fears, negative self-belief, and self-talk. *Master positive self-talk, and motivate yourself.*

6. Like yourself and love yourself, so that others can too. *Treat yourself like you would a child you adore.*

7.   Surround yourself with successful, positive people, and learn from them. *Success surrounds success.*

I'm going to help you be proud of yourself. *You're worth it.*

Follow the 7 rules. In these following *Ability* chapters, we'll be making sure that you are in the right business, have the right mindset and key skills, and the right energy and beliefs to attract your ideal clients, who will pay you, thank you, and promote you for years to come.

Read this book, answer the coaching questions, and really put the effort in for yourself; and follow links to get the online help, training, and support you need to get out of your own way.

I'm with you all the way, and I am looking forward to being your Business Coach, Consultant, Mindset Mentor, Believer, Prodder, Hugger and Trainer, ensuring that you really do have The Mindset for Business (and life).

And so we begin!

Are you ready to shift?
Go all in to get the most of YOU out.
Come on, let's do this…

Grab some paper and a pen; there will be lots of coaching questions. It will be as if I am in the room with you. Maybe even get a special notebook/journal to capture your deep thinking, ideas, and realisations, and do the tasks. I hate to get all bossy on you, but if you don't do the tasks as you read, then you are just reading another book, and you won't get the best results. Take some time for *you* each day, and work through a chapter a day. It'll take no more than half an hour to get your *Mindset For Business success*. Surely you are worth half an hour out of your 24 per day!

Chapter 1

EnjoyAbility

"We are shaped by our thoughts; we become what we think. When the mind is pure, joy follows like a shadow that never leaves."
~ Buddha

EnjoyAbility: the ability to enjoy your life and business.

Are you enjoying it? Are you?

It's a simple enough question—a bit like, "Are you happy?" *How do we ever know?* We might not know if we are, but we DEFINITELY know if we're NOT!

If you're not happy or enjoying it, you may as well go and get a job (and if you hate your job, you may as well start a business!).

There, I said it—shock, horror. I am likely to say some things that are going to be rather provocative throughout this book. It's how I get my reputation for saying the things and asking the questions that are needed to expand your mind and thinking, in order to SHIFT you from being stuck. Hopefully, you trust my methodologies.

TASK:
On a scale of 1 to 10, where are you currently in regard to enjoying your career (1 being terrible; 10 being euphoria)? Write it down as a starting point, noting your reasons for choosing those numbers... I also want you to write down what 1 would be for you (the worst), and also what ten would be like (probably the dream), so that we know your highest and lowest.

I bet you are not a 10, or you would be living the life of your dreams and not reading this self-help book! In fact, you'd be writing a book yourself, probably called, *How to Have the Life You Dream Of.*

In my experience, personally, and from the people I coach, they're not so much enjoying it as they are being determined and doggedly doing it, and getting up, day in and day out. They are fearful of failure, and are also scared of what changes success might bring. Sometimes it feels like wading through treacle; other times, it's euphoric and there's joy. So, the trick is to make sure that most things you're doing, you're enjoying. Remember, every job has something boring.

It's the 80/20 Pareto principal. As long as you love 80% of your business, then you can abide the other 20%.

(If you don't know what Pareto is, and want to know, please Google it, as I haven't got time to quote other people's stuff.)

If you are not enjoying your business, you have simply swapped one soul-destroying situation for another. And yes, you may have had some crap days in your job, but at least you got consistent money and paid holidays, and time off outside of the 9 to 5 grind... Whereas now, you have disappointing days, not so much money coming in, relaxed time off doesn't really exist, and unless you've got all your systems streamlined, which we're going to talk about in this book series, you potentially feel like you are not doing enough and will never have enough time to finish everything, or anything.

Sound familiar?

Enjoying life—isn't that what we are all here for? To smile, to bring joy to others, and have that heart filled with wondrous joy. So, I'm Vivienne Joy. I can't have joy in my name and not be living it, can I?

I've got an enjoyment-themed question for you.

TASK:
Think of every part of your business, and choose your 10 key tasks. (Yes, a task about tasks.)

Which tasks do you ENJOY, HATE, or AVOID?

On your paper, create 3 columns with these titles, and list those 10 tasks into the correct columns to get the true picture of your day-to-day life. If you are avoiding or hating on more than 2 of the 10, based on the Pareto principal, we have a lot of work to do! *(If you have yet to start your business, still do it with your projected tasks and knowledge.)*

Let's build a map of your joy...

When did you last feel so elated that time flew past? Think about when you were doing something you loved. It was so amazing that you just didn't want it stop, or you didn't even realise the time—what was that? What were you doing?

I'm sure, in your social life, you can find quite a few things! Things get said to me when I ask this at workshops: "On holiday, it just flies past. Before I know it, the fortnight in St Lucia is gone." It could be in your social life, on a night out on the town, or going to the theatre.

TASKS:
What do you really love so much that it makes time fly? Make an *"I love"* list.

In your business/career, what is it that fills you up? Make an *"I'm fulfilled by"* list.

That feeling of, *"Oh my god, it's joyful; I'm full of joy; I'm just lovin' it, lovin' it, lovin' it."*—what is it for you?

Because whatever it is, you need more of it; because the more of that you have, the more you're going to get out of bed and run your business, and the more successful you're going to be—guaranteed!

Do you get it? It's such a simple concept that you might just skim past it.

DO WHAT YOU ABSOLUTELY LOVE AS A BUSINESS. Making money doesn't have to be hard work; it can be effortless and joyful.

TASK:
Think about when you last had joy and felt at your best, and write it down by answering these 5 questions. We are building a picture of your dreams and joy. As you do so, really feel into it, see it, hear it, and bring it to life to remember the details.

1. **"I am at my best when ..."**
2. **What exactly was it about it that you really enjoyed?**
3. **What did you want to do as a child?**
4. **Where did that dream come from?**
5. **Why did you want to do it?**

When I look back at my childhood, it was clear what I really wanted to do.

As an only child, I have always loved being the centre of attention. I loved to sing and dance (still do). I genuinely resented the fact that my parents didn't send me to a stage school; I imagine the main reason was that they couldn't afford it!

I like being in front of a camera. I'm not bad at singing, and I used to be a semi-professional dancer in my early teens (the nearest I could get to the stage). I danced ballroom, modern, Latin, and jazz, and I loved it, until I discovered boys and alcohol and stuff like that. I wanted to be on the stage, to perform; I wanted to inspire, and I wanted to entertain... I kind of forgot that somewhere along my career as a recruiter. I managed big teams and was the General Manager of a company, and then I started my own business. It wasn't until I started to do THIS work, where standing out in an overcrowded industry is essential, that this desire came in handy. I remembered the child in me, the one that did what she wanted to do, not for money and not for anything else apart from it just filling her with joy—she wanted to entertain and make people smile, and to make them feel good.

Your childhood dream is usually related to your real desire!

Most of the people I coach, don't feel good before they meet me! They don't feel good in their lives or in their mind; they've got self-talk going around in their head that is the opposite of joy! It's often very painful for them.

Think about it again... *What is it that you wanted to do when you were a child? If you can't remember, ask a family member or school friend. You'll be amazed what you learn about yourself from your nearest and dearest.*

You may find it has some correlation to what you do now. If you wanted to travel lots, you might find that you're a travel agent (shocker), and you might already be doing it! But if you're not, think about what you loved as a child, and try to bring that joyful child into your adult life. They say we should all act like a child, and sometimes we should (The child shouldn't run the show; let me tell you that much.); but we should definitely have that childlike sense of joy, like when you watch a child and they are literally gleeful when anything amazing happens—they will make little shrieking noises and do the happy dance. Is that you? Do you do that every day? Think about the last time you did that, and get more of that in your life!

TASK:

Put nice, joyful and light music on in the background (Pharrell Williams' "Happy" does it for most of us!)

I want you to write down all the things you can remember that bring you IMMENSE JOY in life. Write down all of the things. Even close your eyes for a while to remember. You should start feeling rather happy! In NLP, we call this a *state change*, and you can create this yourself, at any time! Create a HAPPY MENTAL SPACE.

When you're very much in that amazing *feeling happy space*, I want you to link this feeling and self-talk and vivid memory to a specific word or picture in your mind. You can make a physical representation too, by touching your ear. They call this, *attaching an emotional state to a physical anchor*, or as in NLP, *anchoring*. You're anchoring a new state. That happy, joyful feeling can be achieved by you at any time you choose, by touching your ear and thinking of that word. Try it. Fire up your anchor, and notice how differently you immediately feel. These are your memories; you've just changed your own state.

On your paper, write:

I could get more joy in my business by...

We need to work out how you get more of that joyful feeling, and how to bring it into core tasks...

For me, I love it when I watch a client have an "aha" or an "oh shit" moment, as I call them. Because when they have an "oh shit" moment, they shift. It's really powerful for me (and them), and it's like the BEST serotonin rush! It's as if I get high on it. I do that all day! I get joy every day. It's like an addiction.

We're going to do more of this work. The word, JOY, as you'll probably see, will be in quite a lot of these Ability modules. Enjoy the Ability, and have the ability to enjoy; because when you've got all that going on, you've got a great business—I promise you that. Stick with me, and we'll go through the book, and we'll make sure that you have the Ability in all these areas!

Chapter 2

PossAbility

*"Imagination is everything;
it is a preview of life's coming attractions."*
~ Albert Einstein

What are the possibilities?

What is the possibility of you having everything you ever dreamed of and wanted?

What is truly possible?

You may hear the beautiful, evolutionary saying, "Anything is possible if you want it enough." And then your self-talk goes, "Yeah, right! Well, it would be if I didn't have this, this, this, this, this, and this problem."

You are shutting yourself down from possibility, and keeping yourself trapped with your own self-talk.

We're going to do something now that is quite a traditional coaching tool. You may or may not have done it, and even if you've done it, let's do it, because even if you did it, then things will have changed now.

TASK:
I want you to think about where you are in life. I want you to think about this as a reality check, and where you are right now.

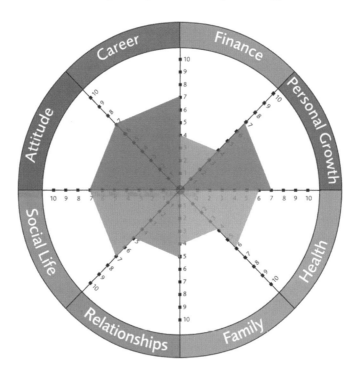

Grab your paper and draw a circle grid like in the diagram. In coaching, we call this the Wheel of Life. Cut it into life segments, *at least* eight, like a clock. Label each segment with the parts of your life that are important; so it could be family, friendship, finances, business, love, connection, spiritualism, health, exercise, or whatever the right label is for you. The grid is just an example.

You can have as many on there as you like. If there are 10 areas, and there's one that you specifically want to address—maybe your diet and fitness and wellness—you may have those as three separate sections, in the way that you eat, the way that you exercise, and the way that you look after your own mental health with yoga, etc.

It could be that you have sections that are bigger than others. It could be that wealth is really important, so you want to actually make sure that that is sectioned too, with property, savings, and other investments.

I hope this makes sense so far. On your grid, put a centre spoke, a bit like a wheel. Label them from one to ten (one in the middle as poor; ten on the outside as excellent). Go around your Wheel of Life and assess it. You don't have to think of any reasons why at the moment; I just want you to assess where you believe that area of your life is. For example, I am on a weight-loss journey at the moment. Therefore, if it was about my fitness or health, it would be pretty low (probably three or four), because I'm really at the beginning of that journey; whereas my business is probably an eight, or maybe even a nine, as I really enjoy what I do, and it's really financially giving me what I need. It gives me the connection I need; it gives me everything I need.

Assess yourself on a scale of one to ten in each area of life. It's like a beautiful way of having a bird's-eye view of your life. The idea is that we should have a balanced circle, like a wheel (hence the name), but as you can see in my example, it wouldn't be a wheel that took a car very far! *Balance is the name of the game.*

Have you done the wheel exercise?

If not, don't do that to yourself. Don't rob yourself of the opportunity. Come back to this module when you've got time and a piece of paper to do it. Don't read it or think you will do it in a moment; you are worth the time now, and it will take you literally ten minutes to do this—and it could change the way you view things, and improve the areas of life you focus on.

Sometimes we're spending too much time in one area of life, because that's the bit that's easy. But actually, the bit that really needs your help is the bit that you're scoring low on and want to improve. We talk about this work-life balance, and everything feeling balanced and in flow. If you've got all these segments working for you, and you know exactly where your objectives are, then it's really clear what you have to do and how to prioritise it.

So that's what we're going to do now. If, for example, you've scored yourself a six, think about where you would realistically like to be in the next 12 months or so. If you think an 8 is realistic, then put an 8, and I want you to join the dots up with where you are now, and then join the dots above where you would like to be, just so that you know what your own expectation is of yourself (*as in the diagram*).

Now we've got an idea of where you are and where you'd like to be—this is basic goal setting. I want you to put the top three things that you could do to get you from where you are now to where you want to be for each section. *With the top three things, you can add more, later, to create a strategy.*

For example, if it were me, and I wanted to get my diet and fitness from a four to a six, my top three things are going to be:

1. Eat and drink clean
2. Work with a personal trainer twice a week
3. Start walking 5k steps a day

Does that make sense? These are real top line objectives. You may struggle in some of these areas, while others will be really clear to you, but at least you'll know where you're in your own way.

So, now I want to do the bit that most coaches don't get you to do, because it's all very well having these three things you could do—but will you? *Probably not.*

There's a reason that you are in your own way with certain areas of your life, and there's a reason you're not doing anything about it. We now need to identify exactly what that is, and rectify it—*agreed?* It could be a variety of things, so let's go through them.

Secondary gain

You may have heard the phrase, *secondary gain*. This is **a benefit** of not starting, doing, or finishing something—a **benefit** of staying stuck.

Sounds absurd, but please hear me out.

Some people like to have something to bash themselves over the head with and feel rubbish about. They have gotten used to feeling like that; it's their version of normal. I once had a client say, "If I did my to-do list to completion, what would I do with my day?" She was keeping herself trapped in the disappointment of not completing tasks, so that she felt busy in her day. Once we worked out *what else she could do in her day*, we unblocked her reason for non-completion, and off she went, getting on with her list and adding to it merrily.

Have you thought about what will happen if you don't change the most important thing in your life?

I had a client once, who was too scared to leave a long-standing romantic relationship. I said to her, "What is your biggest fear?" She said, "Fear of the unknown. If I leave my husband, I don't know what's going to happen…" I said to her, "But you don't know what's going to happen if you stay with your husband—unless you're some sort of psychic, and if so, you should be earning money in a different business!"

The truth is, she didn't know what would happen if she stayed or went, how she'd feel, or what the outcome would be. She was assuming, based on past experiences, and filling in the future gaps. This is a normal thing for the brain to do; it is working out coping strategies. Even our eyesight does it: It stops us from having to see everything, using up brainpower. Eyes see in dots and then fill in the gaps. (Try being in a pitch-black room for any length of time, and notice what you actually see with your eyes—it's freaky.)

Sometimes we're in our own way, and we don't even need to be. We're just scared of an unknown outcome, as we assume that *the known outcome* from the past will happen again. It's the only evidence or forecast our brain can find!

Your unconscious brain believes that THE SAME is safe. I'll say that again, as it is VERY IMPORTANT. Your unconscious mind has been created to keep you alive and protect you (its primary job), and it believes that THE SAME is SAFE, and will therefore try and get you to do the same thing every day. That's why you create a habit, (even if it is bad), because you at least THINK you know the outcome: SAFE.

This is all happening at a subconscious level, by the way. Hence, it is why your *logical brain* will often protest: "Why do I keep doing that when I know it doesn't work for me?! *Sound familiar?* We need to get your conscious and unconscious to play nicely together, and to work together instead of against each other, where you possibly sometimes feel like you are going slightly insane! I know I consistently eat biscuits and then think, "Why did I do that when I want to lose 3 pounds this week?" My unconscious believes that being my current size is safe; therefore, it will do everything in its power (and it is VERY powerful) to keep my body the same size. So, we need to satisfy the brain that *it is safe to swap some things.* That way, all parts of you, and your brain, are happy and succeeding.

The best example of this, which I have experienced myself, was giving up smoking, 16 years ago, in my highest, most stressful time of grief. My unconscious mind thought that I needed it in social situations, where I felt nervous. I identified this by noticing the self-talk clues my brain gave me in the way of a *craving*. When nervously at a 30th birthday party on my own, my self-talk was, "I need a cigarette," to which I replied, "No, you don't; you need to occupy your awkward hands, and escape from this feeling of standing at the bar on your own." I found another way to satisfy my unconscious by going out for some ACTUAL air and taking deep breaths. Each time, I thanked my unconscious for letting me know what I truly needed at a basic level. It worked; I've never smoked since, nor would I.

What I want you to do now is imagine what will happen if you don't change anything on your wheel of life! Take the most important segment, and let's work on that.

For me, with fitness (or lack of it), I've consistently been putting on a pound a month for the last 10 years; so actually, I can assume that in the next 12 months, I would put on 12 pounds. Oddly enough, when I look back to this time last year, I have literally put on exactly 12 pounds. It's my process; it's what I'm doing to stay stuck.

This next task will take longer than those done so far. But it really is worth taking some time over. If I were with you now, I'd be coaching this for half a day. It would be a full-on breakthrough coaching session of setting intentions and aligning them with you. *If you want to do that with me, then do get in touch: hello@MindsetForBusiness.co.uk*

This task/process is about you achieving clarity and creating a priority plan to achieve change in all areas of your life. You'll get some very useful knowledge around the subjects by just doing this small exercise.

TASK:

1. **I want you to give some thought to these questions, and write down the answer... What is your process for not getting things done, or not achieving your goals? What do you do instead?**

2. I want you to go around the wheel now, and think honestly. If you don't take any of those three actions, what will be the negative impact on that section? Will the score go lower, or will it stay the same? Just get a reality check on what will happen if you take no action.

Some examples:

> If you're not doing sales for your business, what will happen to turnover?

> You're not writing the blog, or whatever it is you're doing or not doing to help you in your business visibility—what will happen if you stay invisible?

> Do you continuously take your partner for granted? What's likely to happen if you carry on that behaviour? Is that going to take you closer or further away to your goal of having more success in the relationship?

3. Now we're going to do the other way around. I want you to think about what might happen if you do take those actions. This should be a more pleasant experience than steps 1 and 2! Write those beliefs down as well.

> My example: If I do take some action and change the way I'm eating, and get myself a personal trainer and start walking to energise my body, what could potentially happen in the future?

> In NLP terms, we call this *"pacing the desired future state,"* mapping out the future by the proposed outcome to choose to do it. You're really working it out in your head, and *trying the result on for size.*

Try on the outcomes for each of your life segments, with those 3 action points in place. Do each one separately. Try it on and see if it feels right, because if it doesn't, you will never take action, and I can tell you now that the reason you haven't taken action in those parts of your life is because you haven't believed it, you haven't dreamt that it can be possible, you haven't imagined what it feels like, and you haven't looked back at yourself in a mirror to understand the changes that could be made, and the impact that they could have on your life.

You must also vision the impact of staying the same or the segment getting worse.

If you can see it and you believe it, you will achieve it. The unconscious mind doesn't know the difference between reality and dreaming. Dream often to achieve everything. *It's that simple.*

Chapter 3

Self-TalkAbility

"To love oneself is the beginning of a lifelong romance."
~ Oscar Wilde

Self-talk is the MOST powerful work I do when twinned with belief change. Your self-talk is making you your own friend or your own worst enemy—*this I can guarantee!*

If there are no disempowering beliefs, then there's no disempowering self-talk. No problem!

The goal in this chapter is to have the ability to achieve self-talk that makes you **powerful** *rather than powerless*. If you can achieve this for yourself, and become your own cheerleader, your life will dramatically change!

Debilitating self-talk is like you being your own bully, constantly on your shoulder. How powerfully destructive is your inner bully? That inner voice that says; "Who the hell are you to have a business? Why are they gonna buy from you? You're too expensive! You suck; everybody else is better at this than you are!" Or my favourite... "You should go and get a proper job!" Blah, blah, blah.

I hate to tell you this, but YOU are that little voice! Your little voice is probably saying a whole load of things right now! It probably said a whole load of things before you decided to read this book, and it will be the same sabotaging voice that wants to get involved with other personal development (or any change) decisions too. I can already hear it... "You can't afford it; how are you gonna make the money back? You don't even know what's on that programme! What if you don't have time to do it, like all the other things you promised yourself and failed at?"

I get it; I really do. My inner critic does its best to keep me the same (and SAFE) too. I've learnt to laugh at it, bargain with it, or simply turn it down, like you would the radio, or refuse it like you would a petulant child!

My job in this chapter is to help you be the boss of your self-talk saboteur—*wouldn't that be lovely?* Blissfully peaceful and easy, without that bloody annoying evil voice... I bet that some of the things you tell yourself daily, you wouldn't say to a stranger, let alone someone you loved—they are evil and nasty judgements and criticisms!

Am I right?

This kind of self-talk is what I mean when I say debilitating, disempowering, disabling, and all sorts of really annoying words that keep us stuck in our own way. We all have a self-saboteur; it's our unconscious trying to keep us the same. Remember, the same is safe (*even if it isn't!*).

If you have made friends at all with your unconscious, you might find that your conscious adult mind and your grown-up self is *reasoning with it*, as you would with a three-year-old child... Questions and statements, such as, "What's the worst that could happen? It'll be fine; give it a go! You'll learn how not to do it if it goes wrong, and at least you'll know how to do it next time. Actually, why wouldn't people buy from me?"

Are YOU being your own critical parent? Are you the one saying, "Oh no, don't leave your job; if you start a business, you might fail?" Whilst the encouraging parent on the other shoulder is saying, "Great idea darling; you give it a go, and have a new business. You'll be amazing; you'll work it out; you're smart!" If you have this going on, the chances are that you've learnt that from a higher source (maybe your actual parents); hence, the term, *good cop, bad cop*, in parenting! We learn everything from somewhere. Scientists agree that we are only born with two fears: falling and loud noises—both things that could indicate death... the rest are created by our experiences and decisions.

You would be forgiven for feeling as if you have a split personality at times! These two sides of you are playing tug of war, and in the end, you just STAY the SAME. (So, the critical parent in you wins, as the nurturing parent is hushed by your irrational fear of success, change, or failure.)

There may well be times when the **encouraging voice is in full force**; probably after attending a motivational event, having a coaching session, or even having a great night out with friends, or by someone showing gratitude or paying you. *The empowered you really goes for it!* You step up and you feel amazing! You are the empowered, confident, unstoppable version of yourself, and you are in flow. It's that time when you decide to launch new products, put your prices up, write blogs, record videos, follow up leads, and update your social media. You feel triumphant, fixed, and successful! "Hurray! No need for a coach or anyone—I rule the world!"

But if the **critical voice is winning**, you'll find that you're shrinking and becoming invisible, and you don't even think you're credible, let alone incredible. You'll be overwhelmed, confused, lacking in energy and creativity, and will probably hide and start thinking about stacking shelves in the supermarket, as you start to think that's all you would be good at in this state of mind!

In honesty, a disempowered business owner may as well stay at home and get their mindset on track—your clients will sense it a mile off! Have you ever met someone and thought, "I wouldn't trust them to do business; they don't appear to be on form or have any confidence. They seem miserable and lack lustre..." They are probably listening to the wrong internal voice, so please give them this book, or introduce them to me!

*Right, I hope you get this chapter so far. It is **really important** that you do. The good news is...*

You are not a failure.
You are not broken.
You are not crazy.
You are not useless.
You are not demotivated or any other bullshit that you have been telling yourself for years.

The good news keeps on coming... You are just listening to and obeying the wrong voice. You have learnt your self-talk from somewhere or someone in your past. Anything you learn, you can UN-learn. We just need to rewire your thinking. *Let's do that now.*

TASK:

1. **I want you to focus closely on what would happen in your life right NOW if you could just shut that voice down—silence it. How differently would it feel? What decisions would you make with ease? What would be different for you?**

2. **I now want you to hear that voice that you hear: the negative voice. Is it even your own voice when you hear it, or is it somebody else's voice? Is it like that of your mother, father, grandparent, sister, brother, ex-boyfriend, girlfriend, old boss...**

Whose negative voice is that?!

3. **I want you to remember the last time you said something negative to yourself, and hear that clearly— really hear it, and write it down! What was it? What did the critical saboteur tell you? What might the secondary gain be? What is your fearful unconscious trying to stop you from changing? Write that down too.**

I don't know about you, but if I do something wrong, sometimes I hear myself chastise myself out loud: "Stupid cow!" I don't treat anybody in my life that way; I wouldn't say that to anybody else in my world.

I used to bully myself a lot in years gone by. *Do you bully yourself?*

What do you tell yourself? Do you tell yourself that you're stupid, thick, fat, ugly, useless, lazy, disorganised, the shit one, no good, or that you'll never be successful? These are things I hear when I'm coaching clients. I'm like, "Wow, you say that to yourself?"

Is this you? Is this how you talk to yourself? Be honest. I will ask you now, if you talk to your partner, a member of your team, or a client in the same way that YOU talk to YOU, what kind of reaction would you get from them? Hmm, they would all leave. They would all think you were an asshole, and they would leave, wouldn't they? Yet you are doing that to yourself constantly! It's why you don't like the inner you very much. The inner you is a sceptical, critical bully.

Once you've assessed whose critical voice this is, I want you to visualise hearing that voice coming out of a device that YOU control, like a radio, laptop, or phone, of which you can pause or change the volume... or even a satnav system, where you can change the type of voice. I want you to imagine yourself now saying the nastiest thing that you typically say to yourself (and I'm pretty sure there'll be some). I want you to hear it so clearly—like how loud it would normally impact you, and how you would feel about it. Then I want you to reach out to the device you've created/imagined, and just TURN THAT VOICE DOWN. Listen to it getting lower and lower and lower, and STOP. Has it stopped? And breathe....

Silence. You did it. You did it now, so you can do it every time.

That's the most effective way to stop the negative self-talk. You can do that whenever you want. It's that simple. You can do that (you just did). You're not born with this self-talk, you'll be pleased to know; so, actually, it's you that's creating it, and it's your voice. It's your head the voice is in; you installed this, and you can uninstall it—just like that. You can just turn it down and leave it on mute, or you can just completely remove it, like you would uninstall an app on your phone or your laptop. Just completely uninstall that voice program.

We agreed that if you didn't have any negative self-talk, it would be calm. If your positive voice was the only voice you obeyed in your life, we already worked out in the task how joyful it would be. You now just have the supportive version of yourself saying, "Come on, come on!" The excited one, your cheerleader—you know, when you tell someone, and they're really excited about something you're doing—your biggest fan, saying, "Yay, let's do it!"

Right; now that we have learnt to silence that annoying saboteur, let's get some amazing, empowering self-talk...

The simplest thing I suggest you do for yourself...

TASK:

START SPEAKING TO YOURSELF LIKE SOMEONE YOU CHERISH AND ARE IN LOVE WITH.

How would you speak to a fearful or sad child or friend? Be aware of the tone, the words, the intention, the care, and the love. Give ALL OF THAT to yourself.

Write down all the most positive encouragement you can find, pin it on your wall, and repeat daily to start overwriting the old self-talk.

Rewiring for success...

In NLP, we call it coding. It's the way in which you know how to do something: a plan, your plan, a pattern. In therapy, the term used is **schemas**: schemes of thoughts, feelings, and actions that create a specific outcome.

If we can understand your coding or strategy for a certain behaviour, we can interrupt it, add some new code, and change the outcome, just as you would a computer. *Sounds simple? It is!*

We can also code other people's strategies. For example, if you know someone who is able to do something really well, you can learn their strategy and model it. NLP modelling is used by some of the most successful people on the planet. We call it copying, mimicking... but if you can take the parts of their code and install it into yourself, it then is *your new code.*

Example: When you get out of bed in the morning, how do you do that? I want you to just listen to this for an example of a coding. What happens?

Does an alarm go off, or would you wake up naturally?

When the alarm goes off, what do you think, and how do you react?

It's a question I ask as an example, because I know that successful people have a set code for jumping out of bed and getting on with their day, whilst others wonder how the hell they do that! I know about this specifically, as this used to be me! I modelled it when I was training to be an NLP Master Practitioner as part of my certification.

With my old lazy morning CODE, just the self-talk alone was enough to make me realise I was screwing myself over!

Old Code:
Alarm goes off: I would think, *"Oh my God, the alarm has gone off; I haven't slept well; got to get another 10 minutes sleep, or maybe I'll snooze it for longer; I'm not going to get up and do my exercise today; I'm too tired, and I don't really want to do it."* Hits snooze.

Just listen to my pathetic debilitating self-talk! By the time I'd had all those thoughts, the last thing I wanted to do was jump out of bed and spring into the day.

The person I modelled didn't have any of that self-talk! Her active CODE:

Alarm goes off: She hears it and just gets up, and then turns it off.

There was no self-talk in the middle of it at all! This was a revelation to me. If you're like I used to be, and struggling to get up, this would probably help you switch off your self-talk in the morning. These days, the alarm goes off, and I say to myself: "I'm getting up." And there's no self-talk. I just get up. You'll be amazed at how you can change your behaviour in such a simple way.

TASK:
1. **Think of something that you are struggling to get yourself to do.**
2. **Try coding it to understand your process.**
3. **Find someone who is always amazing at a certain thing.**
4. **Ask them what they think, feel, and do—before, during, and after—and get their code.**

5.   Rewire their code on top of yours, and see what the impact is.

I have many people *code me* for confidence and public speaking. It is an honour to be asked, so don't be shy.

To summarise: You are not born with negative schemas, and you're not born with negative self-talk. I'm really hoping that turning the volume down is going to help you, and I want to ask you a couple of questions before I leave you with this chapter.

The biggest favour you can do for yourself is to STOP telling yourself things that are not true, and start telling yourself that anything is possible. If you have to say that to yourself a hundred times a day until you believe it, do that! There will have been lots of times when people have told you things that aren't true, and you've believed those things, haven't you? If you're going to talk to yourself about things that you don't even know are true, tell yourself positive things... as many of them as you can think of!

YOU be the one that is the power of influence in your life; turn THAT empowered voice up loud, and make sure you keep the other one on mute!

TASK:
How has your old self-talk impacted you until now?
Are you creating the best version of yourself with your NEW self-talk?
Write a list of all the empowered things you have said in your life (to yourself and others), and add to the list the things you will say. This is your new self-talk. Enjoy and practice daily (just like you used to with the negative stuff). Rewire yourself daily.

Hearing, feeling, and seeing, is believing and achieving!

Chapter 4

BelievAbility

"Turn your wounds into wisdom."
~ Oprah Winfrey

I'm not mincing my words with this chapter. It is the ACE of the pack! There are some powerful, deep structure questions to get us really going for it, and you'll soon understand what it is all about.

Your beliefs rule EVERYTHING.

TASK:
Do you believe in you?
Do you believe in your business?
Do you believe that you are the best person for your business?
Do you believe that your business is the best thing for your potential prospects?
Do you believe that you offer value and results?

I ask these very serious questions because, let me tell you, if you have all of those intact, and you truly do believe them, nothing will stop your success! When you believe in yourself, and you believe that you've got the best business, and that your business is the best for your prospects, you will go out and promote and market that, and be as visible, credible, and buyable as can be! People will really listen to you. *They will feel your certainty.* Certainty is SAFE!

Certainty is what we all crave in life. We crave this as a business owner, a prospect, or a customer. It's why *guarantees* hold so much power. It's why we get married, buy a house, and anything else that you can think of that is commitment. We commit to what we believe in, and we believe when we are certain. We become certain by seeking evidence. Today's business evidence is mainly by form of social proof and first impressions that are made in a heartbeat. Our society is quick and plentiful, with millions of sales messages flying toward us. When we feel certain that we need it, we buy... in business, in life, and in love! *No certainty, no commitment*, which in business terms means, *no certainty, no sales!*

If you don't already believe in all those things that I just asked, we need to understand exactly why. They are absolutely essential. I'm sure you'll agree!

Firstly, I want to help you understand what you believe and why you believe it. *Would that be useful?*

TASK:
I want you to imagine that you wake up tomorrow morning and something has happened in the night to your subconscious mind: It has been wiped/erased—a bit like the hard drive of a computer. Empty, factory reset...

What would you believe?
How would you know what you liked or disliked to eat, drink, or wear?
How would you know what you were good or bad at? How would you know what you feared or what excited you?

It was a trick task... You wouldn't know, and you wouldn't remember, as it is NOT instinctive. You would have to re-programme your subconscious mind again—*just like you did as a child.*

In simple terms, your subconscious is the part of the mind that stores all the information that's coming at you. Thousands and thousands of bits of information are coming at you every day, every second. At any given moment, you're remembering how things feel, how they sound, how they look, how they smell, how they taste, and how your mouth tastes at that time, and you're linking them all together in a massive great library of everything you know. It's all completely unconscious, the same as blinking and breathing. Your mind is an amazing machine, operating your autonomous body functions: reproducing cells, thickening blood, and desquamating skin.

Your subconscious is like your own **fully stocked life library**: It has a unique filing system. You speak to your library, with your conscious mind, in a way unique to you—it is your own way of getting access to information. You will choose how you recall information. It's called, in NLP, *your representation system*; it's the way you like to *represent that information back to yourself (and others)*. Some people will often remember how things looked (we call them visual); some people remember how they felt (kinaesthetic); and some choose to re-hear things (audio). Some like to work with just thoughts, and we call those audio/visual, or AD for short. These are the deep thinkers who are very hard to read (and are excellent at Poker!).

If I ask you to think about your favourite song, you will more than likely be able to hear (audio) the song, and the beat and the words; you might even see the artist performing it in your memory (visual), and if you were seeing it as a live concert in your memory, you would remember how you felt at that time (kinaesthetic). Add then the temperature, and even the smell in the air, and the taste of the drinks you had. This is full use of your sensory perception; it is why music videos/live music is so powerful!

You can access all of those. In NLP, we call it VAKOG: visual, auditory, kinaesthetic, olfactory (smell), and gustatory (taste). If it was a really powerful memory, you could remember with all five of the senses; but normally, we tend to represent it to ourselves with our favoured one. When I am working with clients, and they remember an experience in technicolour, with high details, and they have emotion attached to it, I KNOW that a deep belief (or schema) was created at that time. It's how I can go so quickly to the point of inception, and rewire it. It's powerful stuff, and it creates lasting change, as we are working with the master source—the unconscious mind.

The conscious is just the surface. Many unqualified coaches or mentors will work with surface evidence and current behaviours, not ever getting to the core, and that's why sometimes their results don't last. **You have to go deep, and find the first or worst experience,** to understand when and why the schema was created by the unconscious. That way, we can reason with the unconscious, to update the schema/belief, to be more fitting with your life goals and needs today.

How does this happen?

As powerful and capable as the mind is, it sometimes gets a bit confused, especially when there is a RED Alert going on in the system (think anxiety, fear, and depression), or there is an inaccurate belief in there, or some shitty past experiences. The millions of bits of data go through a generalising, deleting, and distorting process to speed it all up. Each time you see a cup, your mind generalises and files it under cup, and that way it doesn't have to work out what it is every time it sees a new object. It's how a baby learns. You show it a cup; you say cup. The baby feels the cup, and the brain creates a file called *cup*, with a schema of how to behave with a cup (i.e. pick it up, fill it up, could be hot/cold, put to mouth, drink, swallow, put cup on flat surface, etc.). If your brain had to create a new schema for everything you saw, felt, thought, and heard every day, you wouldn't be able to operate at the speed that you do.

How your INCORRECT beliefs/schemas get formed, based on this natural process...

Martin says to you, "Oh, hello; you look well!" Your brain searches for a schema or belief to know how to respond.

Let's say that you had just been ill. Your brain would call up that file and create a suitable response: "I feel much better now, thanks." If you had recently lost lots of weight and felt good about it, you would say, "Thank you; I've lost lots of weight." However, if you believed that Martin's thinking, "Gosh, she looks well," meant "She's put on weight *(based on **your belief** about being fat),"* you would say, "Oh, yeah; I have put on some weight, but I'm trying to lose it," and you would feel offended and self-conscious.

Your response is based on your OWN SCHEMA and map of the world, based on your beliefs, your fears, and your experiences, **NOT on the actual comment**, which could have meant anything. Martin would have accidentally triggered a negative belief in you.

Hopefully, you can understand from this simple example that the same bit of information can have a different impact on your thoughts, self-talk, feelings, and actions/reactions. Sometimes you will distort it to fit your own schema, and might not even hear the positive intent in a statement (poor Martin!).

Sometimes, to make OURSELVES RIGHT IN OUR OWN MINDS, the subconscious will completely delete other evidence. The subconscious has a job to do. Its job is to be right all the time, and to continuously gather correct evidence for the filing system, to prove itself right. Hence, so many heated debates and differing opinions in the world! It explains how you can inadvertently upset someone, or cause friction, especially if you hit a core belief or fear point (a real hot button). Fireworks can fly, like a full-scale defence operation. Hence, the statement that some people hear only what they want to hear!

TASK:
Think about the last time you were involved in some emotional upset.
What really triggered it?
Who said what?
How did the other person respond?
Did somebody misunderstand someone?

Many situations can be avoided by simply saying, "I'm sorry, I didn't mean to upset you. Can you please help me understand more about it?" (Then, just listen.)

A common response to the "Oh, hello; you look well!" conversation is one of self-doubt. "Didn't I look well the last time you saw me?" Or, "Oh, it must be this outfit then." This is simply the way the receiver has distorted the information. What the intended purpose of that statement was, is not actually relevant once this schema is in play. The self-talk and feelings will take over any logical reasoning. *There is no logic attached to emotions.*

Sorting a schema

Imagine if you could just wipe out your history and start again, just bringing in the good schemas. The good news is, *you can*—right now!

The things that you're believing will either help or hinder you—*which is it?* I suggest there's probably a bit of both.

How do you know what you're believing right now? How did you decide what to believe? You didn't; your unconscious did, so that is where we have to do the deep change work—in your unconscious.

I've got a unique system that I teach to people to shift their beliefs. It's called the Schema Override System (SOS). Would you like to learn it? *"Yes, Vivienne, just get on with it!"* I hear you say.

You have countless amounts of schemas, many of which are perfectly fabulous and work well for you. They're as essential as oxygen. They are created when you first experience something: the first time you were bored, anxious, scared, sad, or afraid—the full range of emotions. It's all very perfect until at some point we learn something that isn't true, and we keep it as our own *unproven belief*, and then have to evidence. We search for evidence, AND MAKE IT TRUE AT ALL COSTS! E.g., If I believe I'm fat (no matter what my size), I will make sure I'm fat in real life to evidence it.

SOS TASK:
I want you to think about something that you definitely know that you believe, and that you'd rather not believe. It is your negative schema to overcome.

When did you decide to believe that?
Was the belief that you created back then, true then?
Is it true NOW?
What would you like to believe instead, and can you evidence the new belief?

Examples of the Schema Override System...

Many of my clients initially believed that they'd never be rich; they believed that they couldn't charge hundreds of pounds for what they do. My first coaching question, and one I ask you now about your belief, is...

When did you decide that?

Your unconscious might show you exactly when and what happened to create that schema/belief, like zooming you back in time to the memory, to show you the movie (you may even be the star in the movie, or you could be in the memory as you would have been the day it happened.). You may feel some emotion around it, and you will definitely have strong recall of detail, in one or all of VAKOG: how you felt, what you saw, what was said, and the impact.

Now that you have more information around the schema inception point, the next question is: Was the belief you created true back then? It is important to ascertain if it was ever true (9 times out of 10, they aren't). You may have decided something when you were eight years old, which would have been right when you were eight years old, but now, aged whatever age you are, it's probably not true NOW.

My SOS Personal Example:

Schema/Belief: For years, I believed that I was no good at handwriting.

Inception Point: Mrs Parsons, a very tall and overbearing teacher, taught me, the little five-year-old, *trying-to-learn-how- to-write* child. When she first came to my desk, she looked at my writing, and she gave an unapproving look. **My assessment of the way she looked at me was that my handwriting wasn't any good**.

Was my assessment and belief that was created, true? *Was it even true then?*

No, it wasn't. It was my fear that created it. She was probably thinking something completely different—who knows! She might have been looking at my shoes for all I know! I distorted the experience, and created a negative schema. I let that stay with me for years. For years and years, I didn't think my handwriting was any good; I even tried to copy my friend Beth's handwriting at school. So, you understand the impact on me of that schema! And it was never even true in the first place. Even if it had been true, and I could really evidence the experience, is it true now? NO.

It doesn't really matter to me what my handwriting is like now. It's not one of my big deals; but actually, my handwriting's okay when I put some effort in, and I mostly type!

The fourth part of the schema override system is: What would you choose to believe instead?

You just heard mine; and right there is my new belief. It's like a belief update: "My handwriting is OK when I put some effort in."

I want you to think now about the negative things you believe. Write them all down, and do the above task for as many of them as you can. These disempowering schemas are about to leave!

Your beliefs might start with...

"I believe that I'm no good at..."
"I believe that I can't ever..."
"I believe that I couldn't..."
"I believe that I mustn't..."

TASK:
Start a sentence with, "I believe," with a piece of paper and an open mind, and just see what you start to write.

Once you've written them all, ask the 4 SOS questions (the override system) with every single one of them.

You can even do it with the positive beliefs/schemas. Sometimes it's good to find DEFINITE evidence of how awesome we are! Also, if we can work out why we feel so positively about something, we can work out why we love it, and get MORE of it. Get more of what you love in your life—get obsessed with finding, having, and enjoying JOY!

I also want you to think about **where that belief is physically**...

To give an example: When I first thought about my belief about my handwriting, and somebody said to me, "Where is it?" I thought, "Oh, it's actually here, right in front of me." Weirdly enough, the memory could've been anywhere. Sometimes it's outside of yourself, as if you can visualise it next to you, above you, behind you, big, small, coloured, black and white, moving or still... Try *moving the memory* further, or to a different position outside of you. We call these qualities *sub-modalities,* in NLP. Try moving them, and see what happens to your belief. It will shift—isn't the human mind extraordinary!

Play with the sub-modalities, like it's a game! Try this... *I'm giving you all my coaching tips here!*

If the memory is really close to you, by just moving it behind, you'll be amazed at the difference it can make.

If the memory is really massive, just shrink it down.

If the memory is really noisy, turn the volume down.

If something feels really overpowering, just push it away.

Changing sub-modalities is how NLP coaches, therapists, and hypnotherapists often help people give up smoking, and chocolate, and all the things that people believe are so powerful in their life. They disempower the schema.

There's really only one powerful thing in your life: your unconscious mind and how you master it.

Do the SOS exercise as often as you need to. I hope this overview of how beliefs are made has been helpful. You might just find that by sorting out some of your earlier beliefs, your thinking around business tasks shift too.

I wonder, if I'd chosen to keep my handwriting belief, if this book would have ever happened!?

Chapter 5

AccessAbility

*"It's not the events of our lives that shape us,
but our beliefs as to what those events mean."*
~ Tony Robbins

How easily accessed are you? How easily are you influenced?

Do you believe someone else's opinions and judgements over your own?

How easy is it for someone to affect your state, to change your mood, bring you down, or make you angry or upset? How easily are you affected by your surroundings, the outside world, and people?

I use a phrase that I once saw and liked, from a motivational quote… **"Be unfuckable with."**

This sums up how you need to live your life, staying in your own lane and not being easily influenced, keeping your beautiful state, and living your best life.

If (and when) you completely stand in your power and believe in your business and yourself, you are *unfuckable with*. Nobody can access your Achilles heel, your mind, your heart, or your energy. It's all impenetrable— unfuckable with.

Is that you?

When something a bit dodgy comes your way, do you sway dangerously?

Imagine a tree. Imagine the roots of the tree, which are so strong, like the foundation of strength, confidence, and capability of that tree. They are so strong that it wouldn't matter what was going on outside. The wind can blow, the rain can pelt, and the heat and snow can do their worst. The tree may lose its leaves and get a bit of a battering, but the foundations stay strong; it recovers and re-grows.

Are you that person?

Are your foundations strong?

TASK:
On a piece of paper, write at the top...
"When I have strong foundations, nothing can uproot my mood, not even..."

Then, list the things that would have previously knocked you off balance. This is you finding out your sensitive points and hot buttons—really getting a sense of yourself.

AccessAbility is also about tapping into your own genius—the best version of you. Believe it or not, you have a lot of genius inside you. You are a genius. There'll be some things you do, and you will think, "I'm a genius, and didn't even know I could do that." Then, another time, something interrupts the genius state, and you get a bit stressed. Your thoughts are then being structured in the wrong way, like you're not thinking straight; you're in what I call **the red zone**. In the red zone of decision-making, we don't access the power that we have. A part of our power has been tripped or stripped—we see red (fear, danger, or anger).

The trick to a happy life is to change that red zone state to green as quickly as humanly possible! It sounds easy, but it's not so easy to achieve whilst in the red, until you decide to live your life in a beautiful state, and to know how to get yourself back there when life sways you (which it will).

In NLP, we call it a *changing,* or *keeping correct state*. It's vital. It's all about the state you're in. If you're in the right state, then anything is possible, and everything feels in flow—green! If you are in a red state, then anger, frustration, fear, poor decisions, and feeling like crap is what is defining you.

Let me show you how this works in real life…

RED STATE

Imagine now, you're driving to a meeting and you're late. You are in what I call *the late state* (another phrase for red). You're late and in a heightened state of *"hurry up everyone."* You are cursing, fretting, and driving too fast. A car pulls out in front of you, you brake sharply, and aim the cursing at the other driver, and a rising road rage is present. You hit some red lights, and you have more road rage. By the time you reach your meeting, you are in a red state: stressed and annoyed!

GREEN STATE

If you're NOT in a late state, you could even be enjoying the drive. The weather is good, and your favourite radio channel is playing your favourite tune. You turn the music up and sing along whilst smiling to yourself. It's good to be alive on a day like this. A car pulls out, and you think, "Bet he's running late; he should have left more time," and you might tut smugly at the car pulling out; or, if you were deep in your own thoughts, you may not even notice. And in your NON-late state, traffic lights are a normal part of the drive, and you wouldn't even notice them. You would arrive calmly to your meeting, and be deciding what type of coffee to order.

The same journey, the same events, just a different outlook and reaction, all caused by your STATE.

Your internal state creates your external state. It's a bit like going to a business-networking event. Think about when you arrive; what state are you in? What accessed state do you have? Think of your state of mind as different heads. If you had different heads, you could just pick up and assimilate a desired state—wouldn't that be powerful!

Think now of the different types of states you could and would assimilate to have a blissful life… We also call these moods.

Here are a few of mine:

A listening state – when you really need to listen to your partner or a prospect
A learning state – great to wonder and be curious to get new information to train your brain
An action state – when you need to get things done and be really focused and motivated
An affectionate state – when you are just there to care for somebody
A confident state – where you can stand up in front of groups of people if you had to, and talk about what you do, with absolute certainty.

TASK:
Write on your paper, some of the empowered states that would be useful in your life to handle different people and situations, or to get a task done.

Would you like me to help you create these states for you? *It's quite easy and very joyful.*

You need some imagination though, so I hope you have a bit of that, and some visualisation capability. Let's give it a go. Find yourself a nice, quiet, undisturbed space (make sure you're NOT driving or needing to concentrate).

TASK:
Anchoring a NEW desired state... I want you to think of a time when you were totally awesome and felt AMAZING.

It doesn't have to be business; it could be anything: like winning a medal, getting a big contract, finishing a triathlon, getting married, someone telling you they love you, or any time when you just felt truly amazing!

Really focus now. You'll remember the best time. You'll know the one I mean, the time that is fantastic for you. As you bring back every detail, you'll feel it start to come back to you in glorious technicolour. You'll start to feel great, just like you did then. If we could see your face during this process, we would see your face light up and your mouth start to smile... You may even have some pride and gratitude.

Let's deepen that amazing memory. Remember how you felt, how it all looked, how it sounded, what you could see, how you felt... Close your eyes and imagine that time again from start to finish. I want you to be there, as if you're literally there again. Place yourself in the memory as if you're seeing it as a film. Now, step into the film and place yourself in there completely. Associate fully with it, feel exactly how you felt then, imagine everything around as it sounded, then remember everything that was going on around you, the vista of it, who was there, and what you were wearing. I want you to look at your feet in this film, and make sure you're fully there.

Once you have that memory in full flow, I want you to turn it up a bit, and then a lot! The brightness of the vision, the feeling, the intensity and the sound, saying to yourself again the things you said

back then! When the whole thing feels *larger-than-life*, take your thumb and your forefinger, and I want you to squeeze your left ear lobe... anchoring in all those lovely, amazing thoughts and feelings. Also, give the whole memory and beautiful state a POWER WORD... when you feel like you have got the right word for yourself, open your eyes and remove your hand.

Feeling good?

In NLP, we call this *anchoring*. We're anchoring a state that at some point when you're not feeling quite so good, you can think of the word, grip your ear lobe (just as you did), and fire up that anchor, and all the visions, noises, and feelings that go with it.

It works a bit like music, a powerful memory, and state anchor. Have you ever heard music, and all of a sudden you'll remember a time when you were in a nightclub or a restaurant, or at a festival, or in a certain situation. For example, how amazing you felt at that festival/concert when you saw whoever your favourite artist is. What happens is, you don't just remember that thing; you recall everything around it, and all of a sudden, you can get really high and excited again.

We are manually replicating this, except with a physical anchor (instead of audio), so that you can fire it off whenever you need to. You don't have to use this, but I've given it to you, so you may as well.

You can use this anchoring technique to create each of the DIFFERENT STATES you listed earlier. Simply remember a time when you **naturally felt that way**; remember it vividly so that it feels, looks, and sounds as it did back then... and then, attribute a power word and a physical movement to it, and it's yours for life.

You could create a state for anything in your life and have them anchored all over your body! For example, if I want a *concentration state*, where I really need to concentrate, I remember a time when I really was fully focused, bring it to life in my memory, and then scratch the back of my neck and attribute the word, FOCUS. I've pre-programmed that state in myself so that next time I'm procrastinating or avoiding, I fire up that state with the word and the neck scratching movement, and my unconscious remembers that state.

I hope this is making sense to you. I want you to test it now. I want you to do that to your ear, and say the word you said in the anchoring task, to bring back that amazing feeling that you just had. If it doesn't feel as amazing as the real thing felt, you can go through the task and do the whole process again, and just turn it up even more. Turn it up so that it's amazing, and just keep doing it to embed that state for yourself, because when you're in that genius state—that amazing feeling, that power place—then anything is possible, and you can set up as many states as you like.

I have a public speaker state. When I go on the stage in front of whomever I'm speaking to, I have a speaker state. It's actually a breath state. Those of you who have seen me speak or watched me on video will probably notice it now! Running events can be quite stressful, especially when you want everyone to have an amazing time. As soon as I get to my spot where I am on the stage, I'll just ground my feet, narrow my eyes slightly, and drop my head. My breathing goes down into my feet, my arms go next to my side, and I automatically get into my speaker state, because I've *pre-programmed it*. I am then calm and relaxed, which is essential to gain credibility on stage.

You are welcome to borrow my speaker state! In fact, you can do this with anything. Have some fun with it. It's your state, and it's your life; go and be a state creator to be more in control of your mood, and stay unfuckablewith!

Chapter 6

VulnerAbility

"When people are like each other, they tend to like each other."
~ Tony Robbins

The ability to be vulnerable, to yourself, in your life, with your prospects, with your partner, and in any part of your life and business, is vital!

Vulnerability is where you bare all and give away part of yourself, which until that point, you've maybe kept hidden.

I've had many big lessons with this throughout my career! If you have high levels of credibility (i.e. you're bloody good at what you do), sometimes people don't feel the reality of you, the humanity, the genuine-ness (not sure it's even a real word, but sounds fitting), your congruence, connection, compassion, and your real life; and that is not good.

Vulnerability is what people really connect with. No vulnerability, no connection. And in business, no connection, no audience, and no clients means no sales! **Learning vulnerability in your marketing, and with your clients, is critical.**

When you're vulnerable, other people (think clients, prospects, friends, loved ones) feel they can be vulnerable too, and that's how you get an amazing deep trust and sense of knowing someone—that heartfelt connection. So, if you're not allowing yourself to be vulnerable in your visibility and your marketing (and your life), then you're missing a big trick to connect.

We can often do this *sharing of ourselves* more easily when we're face to face. We naturally build rapport with people we like; we seem to *auto-connect* on the level that's right for that relationship, and create a mutually enjoyable exchange. But when you're doing this in your marketing, how do you replicate that? Many people are scared to be vulnerable (or even visible) as you don't know who's watching, or what they are thinking. There is no reaction to feed off, and no interaction; it is harder.

Your marketing activity will be targeting the people that you want to attract and work with; but you don't know how they're perceiving you, how they're feeling about you, or how to create any kind of response/reaction, or action (re-action). What you really want is for them to *buy your stuff*, *join your list*, like, comment, share and take notice, so that they come to you when they have a need that you service. To achieve this, you need to create an emotion. You **MUST** create emotion. The emotion, *motion*, is movement, which creates action, which in business, means leads and sales!

If you're posting videos and marketing that is very credible and corporate, but hasn't got the REAL YOU in there, then you are definitely NOT connecting when you could be! You're missing a massive opportunity!

Think of the marketing channels, opportunities, and social platforms that we have available today: Facebook, Twitter, Snapchat, LinkedIn, Instagram, and YouTube (as in 2019, I'm sure, in the future, when people are reading this, there will be even more, and better and bigger)—but you get what I'm saying. On these platforms, you can be there as often and as boldly as you choose! You can literally just click your phone, look at the camera lens, and say whatever you think and feel whilst pressing record, and then upload and gain instant attention.

What tends to happen though is that somebody records a video, or blog, or something where they're a bit vulnerable, and they start to rant, cry, or to lose control of their emotions. Usually, this means that they are still connected to the emotion and are too vulnerable inside. You may carry a belief that you don't want to appear unstable or emotional, or to depict a non-recovered, unreliable, or uncredible version of you.

Being vulnerable doesn't mean that you're not credible. In fact, it tends to be the other way around! Think about the people you connect with... Let's take *Brené Brown,* who is one of the most watched women on YouTube for the theme of vulnerability. In her talk, she is VERY vulnerable. When you watch a speaker (let's say on the platform of TEDx), in their talk they will typically share part of themselves, their journey, their fears, and emotions. We've all heard the speakers do the *rags to riches* stories: "Now, here I stand, this successful person, whereas years ago, I was living in the gutter and doing xyz, and then I found the answer to xyz and healed myself, and now I'm healing the world." It's really likeable, credible, and human, and it is a vulnerable place to be, and that is exactly what is needed for you to connect with them, listen to their information, and take action. We understand, like, and believe personal stories; we can identify with them.

So, by now, you are maybe thinking, *"Vivienne, I don't have the confidence to be a speaker; I am an introvert,"* or *"I can't do this, that, and the other!"* You don't have to go on a TED talk stage, and you don't even have to do masses of videos (unless you want to; then come and have a chat with me). Marketing is a big variety of visibility. You can start with what you are most comfortable with, and gradually ease yourself into sharing more...

TASK:
Put this book down, write a post about yourself and your "why" in business, and upload to social media—not just on your comfort zone platform but on all of them. Feeling really brave? Do it by video too! Make sure your chosen theme is specific to whatever you provide and promise to clients. If you don't have a story that relates to your business, you need to find one fast, or people will not *feel you* in your business. Even if you sell widgets for a living, there must be a reason why!

Examples:
"I don't know how to do xyz."
"This is how I feel about xyz; how do you feel about it?"
"I didn't believe that I was good enough, but I discovered..."
"I am often scared of xyz; are you?"

I train, coach, and mentor business owners, as I'm doing now with you, in how to be vulnerable. The first place I start with clients is to help them understand who they really are as a business owner, what is vulnerable about them, their true story, and how this can be shared to create impact.

Whatever your business, there will be some unique points of vulnerability that people will identify with and connect to. I would like to help you find them.

To start, I'll share mine with you, just so you get what I'm talking about... I am humanising myself to you so that you feel a sense of who I am and what I stand for. You are deciding certainty and trust, and this is a natural survival process.

I'm a very confident coach, mentor, speaker, author, and trainer. It's probably clear to you that this is my truth. What you can't see as I'm sitting here behind this laptop, is that I'm carrying too much weight, and what you wouldn't know is that it drives me crazy that I haven't shifted it.

A lot of us, certainly as we get to the age I'm at (46 and a half), carry too much weight! We've had way too nice a life and have not taken care of ourselves as we could/should. I do a lot of corporate lunches and dinners. I go out a lot—business networking, speaking at events— and they give me lots of food and fizz; and it's lovely, and I love it... That is my only real vulnerability. I can coach anybody through anything, in their head and in business. I do one to one sessions; I run programmes, ALL IN, where I really help people change their lives, and I give them a complete mindset reset... and yet in my own life, where food is concerned, I just don't seem to be able to do it! It's a real problem for me. I don't seem to be able to stop my own overeating compulsions. I even once had somebody say to me, "Well, if you're such a good coach, why are you so fat?" *(I mean, really, they said that!)* My answer was, "I wish I had a coach as good as me to help me get out of my own way with food!" It really is a vulnerable point for me. It's a point that I'm TOO aware of, and it affects me! I want to look like a beautiful, in- control-of-food person, and I want to stand on a stage and feel good, and not have to worry about my appearance or aching knees.

So, why haven't I sorted this out for myself?

Being fatter serves a purpose for me...

How many people do you know (maybe even yourself) who have this *body confidence issue* as a problem? They're not happy with their hair, stomach, their butt, whatever part of them, their whole body, or even their whole look!? For me to show that vulnerability, it is VITAL. It shows that I'm not completely confident. I'm more like the normal problematic person you can identify with. I've just shared my vulnerability and humanised myself with you, and now, on some level, you will feel differently about me. I'm no longer somebody who is really credible and has *fully* got their shit together. I'm now more approachable, relatable, and real—**all essential qualities of a Coach**... Maybe you can work out why my unconscious wants to keep the weight, to allow me to be relatable.

Makes sense, right?

If you have this as an issue, and are asking why you want to hold on to the weight, it is an interesting question, although that'll probably be a different book, called *Mindset for Health!*

That vulnerability connects, because somebody, probably you, will connect with me and say, "God, yes; I know what it's like to not resist the packet of biscuits, or not say no to the bottle of wine" (glass of wine, maybe, in your case). Being vulnerable doesn't mean I'm weak, does it? It doesn't mean I'm broken; it doesn't mean that I can't help people, but it does show my humanity.

What is it that's vulnerable about you that you can share to help your clients and prospects connect with the REAL you?

TASK:
Grab a piece of paper, and on the left-hand side, write down all your products and services.
On the right-hand side, write the headline of the REAL story that relates to the products and services, which you could share to get connection and interest.

If you can FIND that, and BE that, and GIVE that, then you're onto a winner! You're creating some vulnerability, a connectable story, and you can do that with every platform and every medium—be it video, blog, podcast, events, speaking, public speaking, or a book—however you want to market yourself.

Tip: If you've always got a point in mind of what you're going to say, and you show how you feel about it, then you'll keep the vulnerability in your post *on point*.

Good luck, and by the way, don't be upset if you're a little bit upset when you're sharing your vulnerable stories. I did a Facebook Live in one of my Facebook groups, and I literally started to cry, quite uncontrollably! It was very therapeutic, and the connection that I've had from women (it was a women's only group) was phenomenal! I came off that live broadcast thinking, "OMG, I shouldn't have done that; I should have remained in my state; I should have kept control"... But that wouldn't have been me being real. You gotta keep it real, people! Authenticity is what attracts us to people.... Attraction marketing is all about authenticity—that's what we love, that's what we need, that's what we know! *So, my advice is to let go and be authentic.*

I look forward to getting some feedback from you, so **please connect with me online,** because I'd like to know your vulnerability and story; it will help me to connect with you! Connection is what we all want, need, and crave.

Chapter 7

CredAbility

*"Glorify who you are today, do not condemn who you were
yesterday, and dream of who you can be tomorrow."*
~ Neale Donald Walsch

I'm sure you're sitting there saying, "Of course, I'm credible; I wouldn't have any clients if I wasn't credible"... Or, "Of course I'm credible; I wouldn't be able to start a business, or have an amazing career in my chosen field if I wasn't credible."

I agree with you, and I'm credible too at what I do; in fact, in every part of my career, I've always had a high level of credibility. There's a negative and a positive to that, and we just covered the negative in the Vulnerability chapter (lack of perceived humanity).

The positive is that you become the go-to person... Think about that, though! You might be credible, but are you credible for the *right thing*? Let's look at people like Alan Sugar and Simon Cowell, who appear to have a high level of credibility, but they're known for being... well, I'll let you fill in the gaps of what they're known for being!

I used to run a recruitment-*advertising* agency. Because most people didn't know the difference between what I did and a regular recruitment agency, I was branded as a Recruitment Consultant (not by myself, I hasten to add, but by the rest of the people who just assumed they knew what I did).

Was I a Recruitment Consultant, and just a Recruitment Consultant? No, most definitely not. I mainly got referrals of people looking for jobs and wanting help to write their CV/resume, when what I really wanted was companies who were recruiting. *Totally different market.*

Let's start building your credibility picture…

TASK:
Grab a pen and paper, and answer these 4 power questions:

1. **What do you want to be known as and for, in regard to being credible?**
2. **What ARE you known as with your audience, community, and clients?**
3. **What do people believe about you?**
4. **What do you need to do to achieve the RIGHT credibility?**

Sometimes your lack of credibility in your marketplace is COMING FROM YOU, and how you portray and present yourself! *Sorry to deliver this news, but it is!*

What is your job, title, or business?

When asked, do you say you're a (Marketing Consultant, Accountant, Personal Trainer, Massage Therapist, Personal Assistant, Business Coach… fill in the gap with your profession.)

It is too easy to just sum up what we do, in one or two *industry expected* words! If you are doing this, you are robbing yourself blind of credibility! For every job or business, there is a preconception of what you do, not only by YOUR own unconscious mind, but also by the unconscious mind of whomever you're talking to.

What do I mean by this?

I was at a local business event, about 6 years ago, and there was a fabulous woman, named Becky Adams, delivering a fascinating and amusing talk. She used to run a very profitable UK brothel (yes, you read that correctly), and was talking about this subject of perception. She got me up at the front of the room with an estate agent and an accountant... We all stood slightly nervously as we had no idea what she was going to say or do! Becky addressed the audience for an active discussion. "So, what is the pre-conception of these as careers?" I was first, and I got a bit of a roasting—I'm not going to lie! It was like: "Recruitment consultants never call you back; they lie about jobs; they don't negotiate the best salary; they don't put you forward; they don't care."

Luckily, I'm pretty *unfuckablewith,* so I just smiled in amusement, knowing that none of these assumptions being shouted out about *my profession* were anything to do with the reality of me. I'm sure that you must have dealt with a recruitment consultant at some point, and I'm sure that there are very bad recruitment consultants, as there are in every sector. I also understand the pre-conception of having had shit service from recruiters.

But that wasn't who I was, was it? And, actually, my business wasn't even a recruitment consultancy; I'd just been lazily describing myself so I didn't have to explain. I was really missing an opportunity.

My company used to write job adverts and place them, so by me saying that I was in recruitment, which is what I used to say before I got wise to all this stuff, I was doing myself a massive injustice, and also not allowing the credibility factor in the head of my beholder. They were already generalising their thinking about me, all of which weren't true! So, I soon swapped it to say:

"I help companies to advertise jobs online." And when they said, "Oh, so you're a recruitment consultant?" I'd say, "Oh no, no, NO... A Recruitment Consultant sells candidates for a fee, and there's a big difference. The fee that my clients pay me is to **advertise jobs,** and we work in collaboration" (making sure I used tone and pause to deliver the key words in my power sentence).

Can you hear the difference? What I've already done in my new sentence is overcome the perception of what I used to do, and I created a conversation to easily promote my service.

Are you just an Accountant, Mechanic, or whatever you do for a living? What is it you do? Do you undermine yourself? Do you undersell yourself by saying, "I'm a...?" Really think about this, from a credibility point of view.

Are you doing this? *Stop it immediately, and create what marketeers call, "Your elevator pitch."*

Remember my example, "not a Recruitment Consultant," and think about how you can put that into two simple sentences about what you do, to position yourself as the *go-to expert.*

TASK:
Grab your paper, and start crafting your power pitch...

What pain do you solve for your client?

What is your USP?
(UNIQUE SEXY POINT: what's attractive and alluring about your offering?)

What is the difference of your product/service? (award-winning, longer, bigger, etc.)
What do you achieve for people? (promise/guarantee)
What are you not? (E.g., for me, I'm not a Recruitment Consultant.)

Once you've sculpted it, share it and get feedback. Your clients will help you to capture the true essence of why they chose you (and why new people will too).

The other thing that entrepreneurs do, especially when they start out, is that they get themselves doing so many different things, for so many different people, just to make ends meet! *Sound familiar?* It's the "oh sure, I can do that!" approach, and usually for a lot less money than you're worth. I've been there too!

I've coached lots of Virtual Assistants *(if you are one, I love you and couldn't run my ever-expanding business without you)*. These are highly organised and methodical people that offer secretarial and admin services, on a contract of some type, and they typically work from home. They offer themselves to small business owners, which is great because small business owners haven't got time to do everything themselves. I'm a huge advocate of outsourcing.

Every Virtual Assistant that I coach says the same thing about what they do for clients: diary management, emails, etc., etc.... So, I said to one of them, "What happens if there are 10 of you lined up in a room? You're all in the sea of sameness—who would I choose?" You all look the same, to all intents and purposes, looking very smart and well groomed. You've all got the same heading: you call yourself "something virtual assistant," or "virtual assistant services." So, if I need to have a *go-to*, how am I going to go to one of you—how am I going to know which one?

This is where this *niching* thing comes from, and this is what all the marketing experts talk about. And it's not because they want to teach us *niching*; it's because it makes marketing easier, and you also become the credible one in that niche!

For example, one of my clients (who may be reading this) is a specialist in events management, so I said, "You're not really a VA then; you're an Events Organiser! So, talk about yourself as supporting people who put on events, and then people know what to come to you for. Otherwise, you're just going to be doing what all the other VAs do, and that's not going to get you work easily, or bring you joy!"

TASK:
Imagine now that you are in a room of competitors who all do the same thing, and answer the following questions on a piece of paper:

Would you hire yourself?
How do you stand out?
How does anybody know what the difference is?
Why would I choose you?
Will they think that you can do it? (Perception is everything.)
How do you prove you can do it? (evidence)

What do you do to position yourself? What have you done to *elevate* yourself above the sea of sameness?

Do you write positioning articles and blogs for industry publications? Guest blogs, or vlogs (vlogging is video blogging, in case you didn't know that)?
Do you have a book?
Do you work for local establishments?
Do you work with a governing body of whatever you do?
Do you have groups (physical or online)?
Do you have a signature programme or methodology?
Do you run events?
Do you speak at events?
Do you run a referral programme?

Why bother?

Imagine that everybody is paddling along in the sea, all doing the same stuff. You HAVE TO stand out, head and shoulders above the waves.

Your marketing, your niche, and the way you talk to your audience needs to be very different! If you can get yourself to be the *helicopter person*, you're above it all (and I don't mean that from an egotistical point of view). You're somebody who soars above it and is known. Otherwise, you're just going to be scrabbling around in the bottom of the sea, trying to swim for your life and avoiding the sharks. Don't be that shoal of fish follower person—it makes your business as hard as swimming the English Channel!

Do feel free to get in touch with me if you need any further support with this. It's very important.

Chapter 8

CapAbility

"We will act consistently with our view of who we truly are, whether that view is accurate or not."
~ Tony Robbins

How capable do you **believe** you are in life and business?

Sometimes we think we *can't do something*, and we haven't even tried! We have somehow created a preconceived list of *"I can't do."*

Is this you? Think of the things you say you can't do on a regular basis. You might frame it slightly differently, as "I'm no good at," or, "I'm crap at," or, "I wouldn't be any good at."

Sound familiar?

When coaching business owners over the years, here are some of the regulars that make me roll my eyes:

- I'm no good at public speaking.
- I can't write a book.
- I'm not qualified enough to teach what I do, to others.
- I'm not creative.
- I'm rubbish with technology.
- I hate selling/marketing/admin/accounts.

- I don't understand social media.

(Feel free to add yours to the list.)

These are what we call *good old-fashioned excuses* to stay the same (the same is safe, remember), and to keep yourself small, invisible, safe, and skint. The trouble is that being skint isn't safe, is it!

I remember when I first started writing this book. I'd never written a book and, therefore, had what felt like a perfectly justifiable set of beliefs (excuses): "I don't think I can write a book," which sat in perfect collaboration with, "I wouldn't know where to start," and, "Who the hell would read anything I've got to say?"—a perfect little trio of ways to keep myself stuck. It took me three years to realise that they were all utter crap!

The reason I know the many areas that you need to learn about is because I've been you! Once upon a time (and they truly were just rubbish stories), I didn't know how to use the technology; I didn't know how to record videos; I didn't know what I would say, how I would say it, or even how it would be received... I believed I was rubbish at a whole load of stuff I'd never really tried, or learnt skills in. I can absolutely tell you that you're doing the same!

TASK:
What is it that you are thinking you're not capable of?

On your paper, in column 1, write the thing *you can't do*, and then, in the column next to it, simply add the evidence.

There is a big difference between can't and won't! One is a limited belief, and the other is a decided boundary.

*If you are using "can'ts," you will find that most of the evidence will **disprove your own self-talk** and beliefs—you probably haven't even* *tried!* If you haven't tried, you don't know.

I run lots of events for business owners, and I remember saying to the audience, "Who here can jump out of a plane?" A lady put her hand up, and she said, "Oh, I could never do that; I wouldn't be capable." I said, "Have you ever done it?" She said, "No," as she smiled, understanding that her own belief wasn't true—she hadn't tried it. She then corrected herself by saying that she didn't want to—a totally different thing!

All day long, we are saying, "I wouldn't do that; I couldn't do that; oh no, I don't believe I can do that." So, my question right now is...

TASK:
If you believed you COULD do all the things you need for your business to be successful, would you be doing them? Grab your notepad and, in the left column, start writing the task, and in the right column, the excuse you are telling yourself.

There may be some important tasks that you can't do right now *(due to a simple lack of skills and knowledge).*

What are you doing about that? Are you just allowing yourself to say, "oh, I can't do that?"
What are you doing to find out how to do it?
Do you have the skills to know where to find the skills?
Is there somebody in your life that can help you with the skills?
(P.S. I'd love to help you.)

If you're a *can-do* person, you can.

If you're an *I-can't-do* person, you probably just won't, until it becomes too uncomfortable to not do whatever it is.

We will typically do more to move away from pain than we will to move toward pleasure. Imagine if we could create a situation that serves both! In NLP, we call it *a moving toward strategy* or a *moving away from strategy*.

Which strategy governs you? Do you move away from pain, or move toward pleasure? Knowing this about yourself is very handy!

Moving toward>
I want to be able to do that!
I'm going to be able to do it. Won't it be amazing when I can do that!
How can I learn?
Whom do I know that can help me?

< Moving away from *(the most common)*
No thanks; it's not for me.
I couldn't possibly do that.
The last time I tried to do that, it didn't go well. Actually, I have a friend that tried to do that, and they didn't do it very well either—no thanks.

Your strategy is depicted by what your unconscious conditioning is. Your beliefs will govern what your immediate response to an opportunity or challenge is. You are speaking from your unconscious.

Why do the can't-do people *stay* in the can't-do state?

Sometimes we get addicted to a familiar emotion or reaction. The emotion of *can't do* is a powerful one: an emotion of failure; an emotion of stuck; an emotion of, "Oh gosh, I won't actually have to get out of my own way if I don't believe I can do this." It also allows you to stay the same, and to be risk free! *(Remember, the same is safe to your unconscious.)*

We get addicted to the emotional response and the outcome of... *safety.* The emotion that goes with *can't do* is quite heightened, with slight anxiety, which creates a slight adrenalin rush where, for a few moments, your thinking, feeling, talking, and breathing are out of control.

- I haven't got the time (stress reaction as you think of all the things you have to do)
- * I'm not scared, just not keen (brain remembers the feeling of fear, and causes same stress reaction)
- I haven't got the capability (a rush of not worthy, and fear of humiliation, causes same stress reaction)

Do you hear yourself saying any (or all) of those things? Are you addicted to that feeling, and are staying safe?

The most common one I hear is, "I don't understand the business side; I don't understand the money; I don't understand the finances!" If you don't understand the dashboard of your finances, how do you know how much money you're making, spending, earning, or losing? You don't, and this allows you to be blissfully unaware (denial), and also allows you to *stay in the stress* and have the out-of-control feeling, which gives you a buzz, but just not the right buzz.

One of my most successful online group programmes is the "7 day Money Mindset Reset," which clears all the old beliefs, allows a reality check, and brings in the future. Visit www.MindsetForBusiness.co.uk/ to try it for yourself.

I promise you this: There is no better buzz than having a successful business and being able to truly, freely enjoy your life. It is nirvana, bliss, and joy.

I'm going to take you through an exercise now, to remind or reset your unconscious version of how safe REALLY would feel, to update your beliefs and set you free, and create a new addiction and mission... *I strongly suggest you do this exercise.*

TASK:
Get yourself into a nice quiet space. Close your eyes for a moment. Take some deep breaths to assure your unconscious mind that you are safe and can relax. Imagine that the daily thoughts coming through your mind are like clouds, floating in; you notice them and let them float out again, allowing your mind space and freedom.

When you feel calm, start to be curious: What would it feel like to have everything sorted and flowing in your business? Imagine that you have done the work on your mindset, learnt the necessary skills to be enjoying business, and waking up each morning feeling as you want to feel, doing what you love doing... Take plenty of time to imagine the following:

- You understand your marketing, and it represents you online and offline perfectly.
- Your sales process is fluid, with high integrity and plenty of ideal customers wanting to work with you.
- Imagine them saying yes, being excited, paying, enjoying, thanking you and referring you.
- You are managing your business processes beautifully, and the flow of abundant finances allows you to lead your best life.
- What is that life, and how does it feel when you let it embrace your whole being? What can you hear, and what does it look like in your mind right now?
- How do you feel each morning, afternoon, and evening?
- How are your family? Where do you live?
- From this calm, contented, and fulfilled space, what aspirations do you have for the future?

Now, open your eyes, and write it all down—all the good feelings and ideas.

This is the real plan you vision for yourself…. *How does it feel?*

When I got taught how to make this book into an online video coaching and training programme, it went live on the internet, and people immediately LOVED it and had massive shifts.

My reality was then one of elation, *and also sadness…* I realised I'd spent all those years selfishly serving my own fear and not expanding to enable this kind of information to people that really needed it! Had I shifted sooner, I would have helped thousands more to escape business pain and to find freedom and joy. One woman in particular got very emotional as she'd spent a year with another business coach. She had spent thousands of pounds and was no further forward. It broke my heart to watch her in fear. I vowed to get my support tools out, as quickly and as many as I could; so feel free to share this book with somebody you know needs it!

Your mindset is everything. Which direction it is *set in,* creates all your behaviours and outcomes.

At age 16, my first job was in an accounts department. I worked for Volvo Trucks, for 4 years, managing their accounting systems, sales ledger, credit control, and the like; and I was bloody good at it.

One day, by accident, instead of running the month-end procedures and putting a little 'Y' for yes, on the green dos-prompted computer screen, I put the 'Y' in the *year-end,* and the system ran the whole year-end for Volvo Trucks! And not just for our branch, but across the whole company! I was mortified. How much of *"I can't do"* did I believe during and after the 3 days it took the IT manager, Clive, to put it all back to how it should have been!?

I believed for many years that I was no good at accounts, purely based on this one small human error. This belief I carried wasn't true, was it? If I had been like a judge and jury, and had collected evidence about my ability, I would have found 4 faultless years… but my moving away from pain strategy meant that I focused on the negative, the problem, the disempowering belief.

Can you understand how the belief, "I'm no good at accounts," wasn't really true? I was really good at my job. I'd been there for four years, but that one little error made me believe that I was no good at my job.

TASK:
Grab your paper, horizontally, and divide it into 4 columns.

1. **In column 1, write: all your *can't do*, or *don't like doing*, fear declarations that you make to yourself and others—the ones that are keeping you incapable, affecting your capability.**
2. **In column 2, write: the experience that might have created it (a bit like mine above). It will start to create a powerful map of why you are stuck.**
3. **In column 3, write: what was REALLY true then. Your perception or memory may have been distorted over the years (or a bit like mine did, fear will even help us create really untrue beliefs).**
4. **In column 4, write: what is really true NOW (an update; think of as much evidence as you can to support the new belief)**

I often see *"I could never do public speaking,"* in the columns. Many of us had bad experiences at school, where we were picked out by peers; or we had to stand up to answer questions, with teachers who knew all the answers, and we didn't. Or maybe yours came later in life, with work meetings where you felt out of your depth, or even now, at meetings where you are scared of a negative outcome for your income, reputation, or pride. It could have been anything, where you spoke out and it didn't feel comfortable; maybe owning up to something with parents, or you got a bad reception to an opinion, in which case you then would think you're no good at public speaking or sharing your truth and knowledge.

The way we do one thing, is the way we do everything.

This is a saying I truly believe. You'll hear it throughout this book because it's so true for everyone I've coached thus far.

E.g., If you're thinking that you can't do business-related things to completion, I suggest there are probably things you can't complete in your personal life!

I met a woman recently, named Claire, who didn't believe that she could be boss of her business. She genuinely didn't think she could, and therefore hadn't started her business for fear of it getting out of control. During our private coaching session, she revealed that she didn't think she could ever recruit, train, and manage staff, and therefore would be overwhelmed if her business grew. As the session unfolded, she revealed that she used to do a very high-powered job for a big insurance company—she was the manager of a big team! You guessed it: She had recruited, trained, and managed them—she'd done it all before! She'd had a horrible experience at the end of the job, and had been made redundant (the brain sees redundancy as total rejection of talent, commitment, and effort). The horrible experience had left her unconscious mind thinking that she was rubbish at it all—*it wasn't true, was it!* As soon as she realised this, the relief washed over her, and she had tears of joyful realisation. She couldn't wait to leave our session and get cracking with planning her launch... *Another talented person gets successfully unstuck within 2 hours, to weave their magic in the world!*

I call this *mapping across skills*. Skills have been forgotten, taken for granted, or simply left behind with old wounds, like my client Claire had done. This is so common, especially if you have worked in a bigger, more corporate business, and have *left the corporate world*. Often, you leave the confidence, skills, and success behind too!

TASK:
Think about your past career (all of it, right back to your pocket money job); think about the things you did in that job, the daily

tasks, higher responsibilities, and achievements that you can map across into your current/new business.

Even on a practical level, did you have spreadsheets, processes, communications, sales, structures, or strategies that had been put in by that business? *Could you map them across to this new business?*

List all your skills AND ACHIEVEMENTS from all jobs. You'll notice that you start to feel more confident.

So now that we've looked at positive mapping, we need to look at the negative mapping too! You may have also mapped across some of the *bad habits*, thoughts, feelings, and processes that you don't need in your business.

For years, when I first started my recruitment business, I kept a spreadsheet. It would take me hours to update this spreadsheet as part of my month end process. I did it just because that's what the company I worked at before had done, and my *routine brain* thought I should too. I never looked at that perfectly crafted spreadsheet! What a ridiculous waste of time, which I could have spent generating money and joy!

This is your opportunity to understand your capability in your business. We are going to map the resources you need and the resources you have within yourself.

TASK:
Get a piece of paper and create your own organisation chart, a bit like you would if you were in a big successful business and needed to make sure all tasks were being done by the right people.

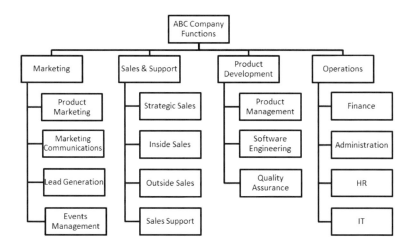

Put the CEO/Chairman/Managing Director at the top; then map down all the different elements that would be necessary if you had a multi-million dollar turnover business (marketing, sales, accounting, customer services, purchasing, HR, etc.). Then, underneath each job function, write down the core skills and personality traits that are needed in your business to do that specific job well. E.g., If you have a consumer business that's online, face-to-face connection isn't important, but the voice-to-voice connection is very important for customer services and sales.

Then list all the key tasks under each job, a bit like you would on a job advert—don't leave anything out. This will probably be ongoing, and something that you work on for a week, or even a month. Every time you think of something you do, write it down under the correct job title. You're creating the job description for each element within your business.

You may find you've done this for the business you have now... MAKE SURE YOU'VE UPGRADED IT FOR THE BUSINESS YOU WANT. It may be that you don't need to be a good staff manager now, but when you have recruited the people, then you might need the skills of being a recruiter, trainer, and manager, so put those skills down on your org chart.

This is the tricky bit. You need total self-honesty...Let's understand the capability and desire YOU HAVE for these tasks. Are you doing them?

Grab a highlighter/coloured pen, and rate yourself, 1 to 5, for each task you have listed for each job.

ONE being: Let's be honest; I'm absolutely useless, have no skills, have never done it, and don't want to do it.
FIVE being: Yep, got that. I rock, I can do it, and I enjoy it.

What you'll start to see is a picture of why your business is where it is. The areas you dislike, or can't do, may well be left, creating lack or unbalance. These are typically finance, marketing, and sales, but it really depends on who you are as a person, what your background is, and your natural aptitude. Once you know exactly where you need to upskill or outsource to get all the tasks successfully achieved, you can get help or training, and increase your capability. If you have identified that all areas need to be covered, then cover them—it's essential.

I hope this has been a useful chapter. It's an exercise I still do when I feel like I'm a bit stuck and out of control whilst expanding my business. It is the perfect antidote to overwhelm. As I scale the business, I will be adding new needs that I need to learn or outsource. PR was the one I decided I couldn't do myself; I didn't have the time, the contacts, the desire, or the know-how... I didn't want to do it, and I needed PR coverage. It was holding my business back. Don't get me wrong; I can put a press release together and find out who the editor of the local paper is, but how do I make sure that they put it in their paper, and how do I contact magazines, and what do I say to these people? I don't really understand the mindset of editors to influence them. Outsourcing this part of my organisation chart was such a relief and made a huge difference to my business!

Chapter 9

ChangeAbility

*"We can't solve problems by using the same kind of thinking
we used when we created them!"*
Albert Einstein

How changeable are you in your life and business?

Are you set in your ways and resistant to change, preferring to stay the same (safe)? Or do you embrace change and in fact *sometimes cause it needlessly*? I'm sure you're going to tell me you are the perfect balance :)

My dad was 74 when he died. He'd been told by my mum and me that he should give up smoking, for five or six years prior. I wish he'd done so; maybe he'd still be alive. I remember him saying: "Oh, I can't change now, Viv; I'm too old, and too long in the tooth. You can't teach an old dog new tricks. I've smoked for 60 years."

It's not true; the future isn't based on the past unless you allow it to be.

The past has passed; it's gone.

The future does not equal the past; the future is whatever you choose it to be.

The past can and does equal the present—it's our blueprint, life script, and map of the world.

I believe that your present life is the sum total of accepting what has happened in your past plus your hopes and fears around the future.

If you have more fears/scars from the past, you are likely to have more fears for the future, as you can find lots of evidence to support the worst-case scenario.

What if you could reframe the negative into the positive?

LIFE: Just because you fell out with somebody you cared for yesterday, doesn't mean you have to remain fallen out with them for life. If you reached out, and you both explained how you felt, you would probably resolve it.

BUSINESS: Just because somebody said no to you in your business yesterday, doesn't mean that person will say no to you tomorrow or next year. You could just handle it/them and change your approach— they may say yes.

Do you believe you can change?

If you don't believe you can, then you won't. If you truly believe you can, then you can and will.

You've got to really want it—you've got to want to change. My saying, *gotta wanna,* absolutely proves true to me every time! I qualify my coaching clients thoroughly before they start with me. If they want to change, I want to make sure they achieve this outcome... This deepening calibration of their decision to change, starts the actual questioning process. The change decision is powerful, especially when the financial commitment follows.

In business, cash = commitment!

People who have been stuck for a while are often running a *secondary gain* with their issues/challenges, meaning that they unconsciously want to keep them; they will not shift until they replace that secondary gain with something more positive. They don't want to change (a bit like my dad). And so the saying was born: "You can take a horse to water, but you can't make it drink."

Let's remember what I said about secondary gain. It's an important concept to grasp.

Secondary gain is a perceived positive gained by a negative.

I hear you thinking: "Vivienne, there is no secondary gain to me keeping my problems! I don't want to not earn the money I deserve, or feel insecure about my business, or not feel confident at a networking event." I hear how crazy that sounds, but none the less, often there is.

Example: Do you ever hear yourself say, "I didn't succeed because I didn't really put all my effort in?" It's a really common self-preservation method to save you feeling like a failure (none of us are keen on that!). If you had a relationship break up, it's like, "Well, I didn't really put my all in, but they weren't really right for me, so it was okay." It's a defence mechanism we have built in. Unfortunately, it often stops us from actually *giving our all*, or choosing what really is best for us; and therefore, we end up failing or feeling totally satisfied—*a self-fulfilling prophecy!*

Have you heard the saying, "Someone convinced against their will, is of the same behaviour still?" This was a hard teaching for me in my early coaching career. I wanted to help everyone. I did my best and couldn't work out why some of the results were remarkable and others not so good. *I now realise I can only help those who want to change.* You can't change other people; they have to want to change.

Our unconscious mind needs to know that IT is coming up with all the solutions and answers. We don't like to think we needed to ask for help *(some of us more than others; I'm sure you know a few know-it-all people!).*

Let's say somebody comes to you with a problem... They tell you the problem. You then launch into what YOU would do to solve it, and you give them your best advice (this is consultancy and mentoring). It is your absolute belief that *your advice* is what they should do. However, you're coming at THEIR problem from YOUR map of the world, and they didn't really believe or agree, even if they nodded politely and thanked you. They have a different map. Or maybe, despite their moaning, they have a reason to stay stuck *(secondary gain).* It's why advice rarely works!

You *gotta wanna* change...

Sometimes people like to be stuck in their problems; it gives them something to moan about! Let's be honest; as a nation, especially in the UK, we love to have a moan! If we didn't moan about this or that, we'd moan about something else. I once had a boyfriend named Lloyd, who said to me, "Oh, I'm glad you're moaning about me not doing things like putting the toilet seat down, because it actually means that there's nothing really wrong in the relationship." He was annoyingly right!

If I'm training or consulting at a bigger business, where they're moaning about something that's really quite irrelevant, then there clearly aren't that many issues. As humans, we'll often shift our moaning from one thing to another. Normally, if we're not moaning about how much we weigh and how unfit we are, how much money we're spending to live, how many holidays we haven't had, how much money we haven't got coming in, the state of the roads, or the economy—and our favourite, the weather—we'll find something inconsequential to moan about, or gossip about, highlighting someone else's problems!

Staying stuck sometimes serves us.

I once had a client named Sue, who was terminally ill. Through working with me around her beliefs and needs, she realised that *unconsciously* she had created her illness. Now, you might say, "How could she create an illness? How was that her choice?" *It was her unconscious way of meeting her basic human needs.*

Before she was terminally ill, Sue really didn't have anybody around her. She had no care, no support, no love, no help, and had no family close by. Her children had moved away and started their own families. When she was diagnosed, people started to show they cared. She had home help coming in on a regular basis, and people were asking after her. She was checked, and she had physical attention, as well as emotional and mental support. She got worse and worse and worse.

What happened to her? How did the situation occur? The unconscious mind, the bit responsible for us having our basic needs covered, deduced that being ill equalled attention, and the more ill, the more attention! The unconscious mind controls your autonomous bodily systems; it has the ultimate power.

Have you ever had one of your children off school due to sickness? What happens when they stay home? Typically, you do too. You look after them, worry a bit, and check them. They get fed special food, they get to watch TV, and they get extra love and attention until they are well… It would stand to reason that a child wanting more parental attention would *run that subconscious program*me *to get the same result*! Being sick equals attention. I know this to be true, as my mum used to do this for me when I was in my early years of school (around 8 or 9). She wanted me at home, as she was lonely. As an only child, I wanted her love and special attention, so I stayed home. We were both happy—the school, however, wasn't so happy! No surprise that through my later school years, I continued this pattern; I perfected it *(I like to be good at things)* and got great at being sick. I had lots of time off with all sorts of *illnesses*... Looking back retrospectively as an adult, I recognise that I created numerous chest infections, toothaches, backaches, stomach bugs, and my biggest triumph, asthma, which served a dual purpose, as I no longer had to do long distance running at aged 14, and was actually often off school for weeks at a time. I hated school due to the bullies, so it served me very well to be sick and safely at home with my mum!

As a young adult, I had to unpick this programme to change it and rewire it. No employer was going to stand for that inner child behaviour and loss of productivity. When I discovered NLP, I took the old programme disc out and put a revised disc in. I loaded the correct behaviour to install the change I wanted. I fixed it. I am rarely ill these days. If I am, the first thing I ask my unconscious is, "What are you avoiding, or what do you need?" It's usually a day off, or some love and connection. I just find a more productive way of having what I want these days, instead of being sick.

Albert Einstein was famously reported to have said, *"Doing the same thing twice, and expecting a different result, is the definition of madness."* And it is.

What is it that you want to change? The first question to ask yourself is: "Do you want to change it badly enough, or do you *just think you should*?" I call this *musterbating*... I must, I must, I must. It won't get you to the point where you change, but it makes you feel like you are in the change process, as you keep declaring it (**false progress!**).

The best example of this is people that turn to hypnotherapy and NLP coaches to quit smoking. They say, "I really should give up smoking."

I'll say to them, "Should you, or do you want to? How badly do you want to be a non-smoker?" Often, they'll say, "Well, I just think I should. My doctor, mother, partner, and child told me I had to." It's not their true desire to quit. Remember: "Someone convinced against their will, is of the same behaviour still!"

This *want* versus *must* is the pivotal question and decision. One is enforced; the other is an empowered choice, where there is leverage, which means that the drive to change is more powerful than the need to stay the same.

No internal decision or motivation = no change.

We are now going to understand your *strategy for change.*

TASK:
Think of a time when you changed something with ease. It could be anything in life or business, and could be good or bad (it is all change!).

Write them down on your paper in column one, and draw 3 more columns (so 4 in total).

Examples of positive and negative past change:
- **Stopped taking sugar in tea/coffee**
- **To go to the gym 3 times a week, and now don't**
- **Decided to change your job and then did**
- **Left a rubbish relationship**
- **Dropped a negative friend**
- **Started singing in a choir**
- **Had a baby**
- **Changed your car**

Column 2: What was your REAL pain or motivation when you decided?

Column 3: What was your self-talk at that time, and the final "that's it" leverage trigger to really change?
Column 4: What did you *actually do*, and what was the impact of that change on your life?

This exercise may take you some time, if you do it properly and really list them all.

You will find that you have a tipping point, a point of leverage, where you can no longer stay stuck—your "Oh shit" shift point!

Very often, you'll hear dieters say, "When I couldn't get into my jeans, that was the end; that was it. I wasn't going up a dress size; I decided I had to do something about it!" That's the tipping point for losing weight!

Another tipping point example is with relationships, when a partner becomes unbearable: "I couldn't deal with him/her anymore. That was it. I had enough. If they can't go out with me for a meal and not argue, I don't want that life anymore—we're over!"

Did you spot your tipping point? If not, you may be a slower burner... Some people just gradually make decisions and shift slowly and comfortably. *Really think about this as it will stop you from trying to change at the wrong pace.* I guarantee that you haven't thought about this *change strategy* before (unless you're an NLP master, trainer, or practitioner like I am; then you think about it all the time.).

Success and failure leaves clues... *The way we do one thing, is the way we do everything.*

What is your methodology? How do you change? Do you put up with things for a long time, and then, boom, you decide and take immediate action; or does it take you a long time to think about it, weigh up, and then you just kind of generally integrate things? There are no right or wrong ways. It is important to know *YOUR WAY*.

If you're a snappy decision-maker, and you're *not currently making necessary decisions*; then you may have some secondary gains running like an outmoded programme in the background. Sometimes I watch people trying to give up smoking, and they struggle because they think they still need it. Once we remove the secondary gain, the presenting problem leaves too, effortlessly.

A few years ago, my friend, Jo, asked for my help, as she had started smoking again in her late thirties, and was desperately struggling to quit. "What is it that you believe smoking gives you, Jo?" I probed. She replied, "A break! It relaxes me when I feel stressed," was her immediate answer. Is it any wonder she was struggling to give up something she believed she still needed! We helped her unconscious realise that it wasn't true—the cigarette wasn't relaxing her—and then went about working out what the smoking was *really all about,* and gave her a new way of relaxing and taking a break.

Jo was going through a traumatic time with her youngest child; they were in hospital too regularly, as she was very poorly with a life-threatening cancer, and Jo was naturally insanely worried. We determined that it was the act of leaving that stressful hospital situation, and going outside for a break, that Jo REALLY needed. Fresh air was just as effective to give her breathing space; it wasn't the cigarette at all that she needed. Having decoded the unwanted habit in order to understand what she really needed, she was able to choose a new method. Had we not done this, she would have tried to give up smoking and failed abysmally, because she didn't get what she needed by just giving it up; there was still an unfulfilled basic need.

Your unconscious mind is on your side; it is there to protect you. It believes that these old programmes and patterns that you're still running from years gone by have a purpose—a very high-level purpose. When you work out your gain, you'll be able to get rid of the pain and the habit/behaviour.

I really want you to get this concept, so if you are struggling, please ask me for help. Once you understand your own strategy for keeping unwanted behaviours, or your motivation for lack of change, you can find the secondary gain, fill it with something more acceptable, and map your strategy across for lasting change.

Change is an essential part of life. You may as well accept it, get some coping tools, and even learn to enjoy it!

Chapter 10

ProbAbility

"Change will not come if we wait for some other person or some other time. We are the ones we've been waiting for. We are the change that we seek."
~ Barack Obama

This isn't some sort of gambling forecast; it's about the probability of you getting out of your own way and changing your life to be a life that you love, are proud of, and enjoy!

Will you?

So far, in this book, we've talked about how you can start changing your disempowering beliefs, changing your destructive behaviours, and understanding secondary gains, to fulfil them with something more positive. We envisioned moving toward pleasure and away from pain, toward the life you felt and saw to be possible for yourself... I'm wondering if you're going to be one of these people who says, "Oh, I get it," and then does nothing differently. Or, whether you will *actually* get out of your own way and change the necessary stuff based on what you have learnt so far.

What is the probability?

Many businesses have good *business coaches*; they do goal setting, work out the numbers, put together a marketing plan, and set the key performance indicators... *then what happens?* Some will do the work rather than get prodded by the coach to meet the deadline. Others don't do the things they agreed to do, and instead, make excuses. They do nothing different, and guess what? NOTHING changes, apart from the fact that they are spending profits on a coach—a frustrating relationship for all parties. *The mindset has to be sorted first!*

Some make efforts and change; others make excuses and remain the same.

If you don't do something to change, then nothing changes. It's a common saying. However, I don't think it is strictly true. If you don't do something, change happens anyway; but not in the direction you want it to go in!

Example: If you felt unwell and didn't go to the doctor, and it worsened and you didn't take action, you could get worse and worse... So, actually NOT taking action WILL change the outcome—for the worse, not the better, and potentially not repairable!

The number one thing I coach with clients Is procrastination and sabotage behaviours; hence, my reputation for getting people out of their own way...

How can we stop procrastination and self-sabotage from being the case for you? Would this be useful?

There are years and years of NLP training simplified for you in this book. I would hate for you to just read my chapters and do nothing different; it's my worst nightmare!

You're spending time and money on this book; we need to make sure that you do the change work. Just thinking about what you want to achieve, doesn't make it happen, *does it?*

There are FOUR basic reasons why people procrastinate and beat themselves up over their lack of action, progress, and success... Here they are with their solutions:

Lack of skills, knowledge, or desire to do the task in hand.

LEARN HOW or OUTSOURCE

The motivation is low; there is low perceived value, and no real WHY.

UNDERSTAND THE VALUE or DITCH it

There is a fear or schema running to keep you stuck.

FIND THE SCHEMA AND RESET YOUR BELIEFS

Lack of goal clarity, no plan, no deadline.

GET A PLAN YOU BELIEVE IN and STRONG MOTIVATION TO DO IT with a TIMELINE of action

Let's do a working procrastination example, and then you can work out what is keeping you stuck...

I often think and even say out loud, "I would love to be really fit and slim." *This is my biggest and most problematic task.*

Just saying it won't make it happen (sadly).

Knowing my challenge, help me work out which of these are the three core reasons that I'm stuck. *Let's do a bit of investigation...*

Do I know what I should eat and how I should move each day? Do I have the knowledge and skills?

Yes. In fact, I ran a business for 4 years, around ketogenic and low carb dieting. I know exactly how the body works.

Am I lacking in a real WHY?

Hmmmm, quite possibly. This level of weight and fitness is known to me; I'm used to it. If I were diagnosed with some sort of terminal illness or life-threatening condition, do you think I'd be more focused on my weight, my eating, and my behaviours around food, exercise, and fitness? *You betcha!* It'd then become a VALUABLE priority.

Is there a fear or schema?

Yes, there is. I believe that people like me better if I'm fatter. Most of us like to be liked, and I'm more approachable and real when I'm fat (is my belief). Is it true? Maybe. Do I need to sort this schema out? I absolutely do, or I will be continuously sabotaging and procrastin-ating to keep myself the same; hence a string of failed diets! In fact, my expected outcome of a diet is failure (might need to reset my beliefs around that too, eh!).

Is there a lack of goal, clarity, direction, or plan?

No, I have had countless plans and goals: "Be 28 pounds lighter by my birthday; be a dress size less by my next mega speaker event; be fit at 40!"

I sabotaged them all because of number 3; and also, I need to make number 2, my real why, more valuable and clear!

Can you see that by doing this simple exercise, I can tell precisely where my blocks are, and can start working on them, by myself or with a coach?

TASK:
Your turn. Write down all the things you would like to achieve but are sabotaging, and ask yourself the 4 steps, to understand what you need to work on. Sounds simple, but it may take you a while.

Your values show you what you value...

Your value set is something that *is set*. It's very hard to change. They are your core values.

If somebody challenges one of your values, you will react to it. When you see an internet troll, fall out with someone, or have a heated debate (a reaction in some way) on social media, this is typically where somebody's value set has been challenged or poked—it causes a reaction.

Your value set is at the very core of your identity. Behaviours come and go, our skill set evolves, our results vary... but our values stay strong, and *they rule everything!*

For example, there's a saying: "Hell hath no fury like a mother scorned." My mother was a great example of this. My mum's core value, the thing she valued above anything else, was *ME*. Her only, precious, joyful child (hence the middle name, Joy).

When I was being bullied at school, at age 12, my mum got a call from the school to say, "Come and pick your daughter up. There has been a bullying incident, and Vivienne isn't safe." There was a group of girls at the gate, waiting to *get me*, and I was so clever (or scared) that I went into the headmistress's office and said, "I'm not leaving; those girls down there are waiting to kill me." My fear-based language distortion amuses me now... they probably weren't going to kill me; really, were they? Who knows—they probably would have called me names and stolen my school bag! *My 12-year-old fear state was terrified they were going to kill me; I'd never been disliked before and didn't know how to deal with it!*

My mum didn't drive, so she had enlisted the help of the trusty next-door neighbour, Bridget, to drive her through the school gates. They arrived in a whoosh of protective anxiety, my mum with a black handbag clenched in her angry hands. I later discovered that all that was in the bag was a huge, great carving knife!

My mum had no fear of consequences of protecting me. She would defend me to the death; she valued me more than anything in the world. That's how strong your value set can be. I'm sure you feel the same about people in your life: your children, parents, family members, and partner, or whoever—you get what I'm saying here.

You can and will feel THIS passionately about all your values. Some of the most typical are religion, politics, abortion, education, border controls, loyalty, integrity, saving the planet, and sports! *Add your own to the list.*

Your value set is really important. It sets up your map of the world and how you believe it should be!

If you highly value integrity, and somebody challenges *your* integrity, the pain that you feel and the way you will react is with passion and power. I'm sure you can remember a time when the strength and intention of your own reaction (or someone else's) shocked you. *Values create passion.*

If something is valuable to you, you will do it—no question, no sabotage—you just do it.

A few examples...

You value your teeth, and I'm sure that you brush daily. You'll never say, "Oh, I'll brush them next week."

You value your children and wouldn't dream of saying, "Oh, I'm too tired to pick them up from school today."

We always achieve what we value. We are driven to serve our value set.

What would magically happen if you found (or created) your core value driver in the tasks/projects you're avoiding? If we linked the success of your tasks to your value set, they would become really powerful, and you would be driven to succeed!

Really successful people have this going on.

To you, they look TOTALLY dedicated, full of passion and energy, and fearless. They have such dedication, they'll work through the night; they'll go and go and go *(a bit like me, maybe)*. Their business is attached to their value set. Think of people who are charity workers; they'll literally work for free, because they highly value what they can do for the community of people that they're working to help.

Let's power up your things to do list...

TASK:
In a moment, I'm going to ask you some questions. On your paper, write down the first things that come into your head. Don't edit the things you write. It doesn't matter what order the information comes out in. I want you to just write down everything.

What do you value the most in life?
What can't you live without?
What is it that you would do anything to have or achieve?
Whom would you do anything for?
If you couldn't have this, you would be dead emotionally, mentally, spiritually, financially, and physically.
What is the most important thing to you?

Keep writing until you have your list. Most people have at least five things, and sometimes ten. If you have any more than ten, you'll find you've got a duplication, and we can group them together.

This is a list of your values and priorities. Some of them will be your core values, but the top three are typically your core values.

I want you to look at your piece of paper, and put them in order of importance. We need to make sure we've got your top three, because they don't necessarily come out in order.

For example: If my core value is relationships, but I've got problems in my business, my head is likely to focus on just the business at this time, especially if everything is fine in my relationships. *Does that make sense?*

Sometimes we prioritise what needs fixing above what we value most. To make sure, I want you to ask yourself, if you had only these top 3, would you be able to survive and be happy? If you had just the top one, would you survive? Shuffle until you have the top 3 in the right order.

Are you surprised what did or didn't come up in your top 3?

I do this exercise a lot during group sessions, and with one-to-one clients. One time, a woman's dog was her absolute priority. As a group, we challenged it, but her dog was definitely more important to her than her husband. (No comment, but there may be a few animal lovers nodding at this point.)

For quite a lot of people, health is up there in the top 3. Without your health, you can't do anything else. Yes, you may be uncomfortable without your partner, children, career, house, friends, your car, or whatever else is on your list... but, if you had your health, you *could* rebuild your life.

For me, health is my fourth (sometimes lower)! Hence why it's not my focus!

1. Connection is my number one. I love to be connected to people and the Universe; it's the most important thing to me.

2. Number two is significance; to be valued and make a difference.

3. Number three, for me, is freedom. (To be free to choose how I spend my time and travel, and who with: free spirit)

My vocation in life is to travel the world (3), connect with people (1), and help them change their world to the stage where they enjoy life (2). My business hits ALL THREE of my core values. It brings me ultimate joy and fulfilment. Yours will too, if you make sure it is *aligned*.

My recruitment business was successful; I changed lives by finding jobs for people (it hit number 2 value). However, I didn't really have the connection with people that I needed long term, and I certainly didn't get to travel; in fact, I was office bound. It only hit one of my values. Now I hit all three, and it is like a different life.

When I'm connecting with someone's innermost thoughts, fears, and dreams, it really gives me that sense of connection. In that total immersion with my client, there's nothing else in that moment—just my connection with them and our mission. It ALWAYS feels beautiful, rewarding, and powerful.

I get messages of thanks and gratitude daily from people who feel their world is different; they are free too. I'm writing this chapter from the French Riviera, and I'm about to fly out to Las Vegas. I will work 16 hours a day and into the night to achieve my full potential; it energises me. I am no one special; I have just done the personal development exercise, and more, in this book. I feel totally alive and valued by the world. I would do it for free. I feel truly blessed to have found my thing, to be exceptional at my thing, to get paid well for my thing, and to get to live my best life—my dream life—that I envisioned (just like you did a few chapters ago).

TASK:
How do you feel about your business right now (new or old)?

How does your business align with your top three core values? Write down, next to your values list, the things from your business that align with your LIFE NEEDS—your complete business, as well as the tasks.

If they are in alignment, then you'll be fully dedicated and happy, and there'll be nothing that stops you. If not, then you need to find a way of doing so.

Let me show you what I mean...

As I was saying earlier, my health is fourth on the list. *Hangs head in shame.* I know it should be much higher; it's really important! Literally, life or death.

When I fully focus on the future facts, *health starts to get a bit more important.* If I'm not healthy, I can't serve people. If I'm not alive, I can't show up and get the connection and help people change their lives. No health, no life, no point!

If I then add in the significance of people's perception of me when I speak from the stage or appear publicly, it gathers importance... If people perceive me to not be in control of my food, then how can I be a good coach, which may stop them from choosing to work with me! (gulps)... It now starts to be fucking important. Really important!

Hurray, I have aligned my 4th goal with my top 3 values. Much more likely to happen, especially when I deal with the schema in place, and reset a clear goal (the other steps in overcoming self-sabotage that we went through).

If you've got goals that you're not sure of, and they're not aligned with your value set, do the previous exercise. If you need some help, then give me a shout, and I will be happy to go through the process with you. It's always a motivational session full of relief and light bulb moments! Most people think that their self-sabotage patterns mean that they are weak, or there's something seriously wrong with them. As you can now see, it simply isn't the case!

Remember that your unconscious doesn't know the difference between the dream state and reality. So, once you've got those goals aligned, and you keep thinking about them in the powerful version of achieving your top 3 values, you will make sure you get there! Just take a moment to once again remember what it's like when you get there. Think about those goals, really think about achieving those goals, and imagine what it's like to feel joyful success.

Chapter 11

LearnAbility

"Once we accept our limits, we go beyond them."
~ Albert Einstein

How open are you to learning new stuff?
When did you last learn anything new?
What is your attitude to learning?

I don't mean what's happening on the latest version of your favourite soap opera, or which celebrity is sleeping with who... I mean for your business. *How open are you to learning how to have the ability to run your business successfully?*

Isn't it annoying when you tell somebody something helpful (giving advice), and they say, "Oh yeah, I know," and you know full well that they don't REALLY know, because they are still not doing what they could/should be doing! It could be that *you've* had a massive experience of writing blogs on a weekly basis, and the impact that task has had on your business is tremendous. You'll say to your business friend, "You should write a weekly blog; it has really improved my audience reach," and they reply, "Yeah, yeah, yeah, I know it would." Aaaaarrgghhhhh!

I KNOW.

It's a little phrase; a phrase that is the thief of all sorts of skill and education learning. It's prompted by the subconscious need to always be right about everything.

When someone says, "I know," the back of the brain just shuts down to learning and possibility. *It's a killer of progress.*

I often repeat a super true saying from the book, *The Seven Habits of Highly Successful People*, by Stephen Covey, *"To know and to not yet do, is to not yet know."*

Think about it. In the *blog advice* example above, the guy who says that he knows but isn't getting audience exposure as he's not writing a blog, **really doesn't know** the power of the result of that activity. *He hasn't a clue, really.*

We all know that we shouldn't binge drink alcohol, because we know that it'll give us a hangover and is bad for our health, so we should stop, but we carry on regardless.

What is it in your business that you're making excuses about by saying to yourself or others, "I know I should?"

Do you KNOW the importance of the task and the outcome of each task?

Think about your to-do list; think about the things you have added. Do you know how to do them? Do you think you do, but really are not too sure? And so, the reason you're not doing them is because you don't know how to! If you knew how to do them, and you knew their importance, you would do them, surely!

Get rid of the phrase, "*I know*." Be open to opportunity and learning. You can learn so much when you don't think you know everything, because let's face it, none of us know everything. In fact, you don't know everything; otherwise, you wouldn't be reading this book!

I want you to be stronger than your best excuses. Which excuses are you making to NOT learn how to get out of your own way?

When I was writing this book, my excuse was, "I don't understand the layout of a book; it's going to be expensive to self-publish." The truth is that I didn't have a clue if it was expensive, and I actually did know how to lay the book out. **So, the things I thought I knew, I didn't!** I knew nothing in fact, apart from the subject backwards! I was assuming. Assumptions will also wreck your business.

In regard to assumption examples, I could go on for hours, but I'll assume that you get what I mean.

People assume that a coach or mentor is not affordable to them, but when they discover the difference, and the level of investment, they realise that they really didn't know.

People assume that you are seeing their social posts and would comment if interested. They probably aren't!

Business owners assume that if people don't buy, it must be price rather than the marketing message!

We don't know what we don't know, until we try, and then we discover...

I like to know as much as I can about my industry, so I go to conferences, training courses, and all sorts of learning experiences, two or three times a month. Do you attend these types of things? If you do, you know you'll come back to your business with motivated excitement, and an energy that's been revitalised; you're inspired and determined with lots of fresh ideas, pages of notes, and tasks to start. About two or three days later, you're back into the grunt and grind of it all, and nothing has really changed, apart from a longer list of things to do, and guilt about not doing it. I call this *shelf development,* rather than *self-development.* If you learn something, and then you don't use what you've learnt, it means you still don't know how to do it! It's like if you go on an online course to learn how to do Facebook Ads to drive more traffic to your website, and then you don't do any Facebook Ads... you may have learnt it, but you don't really know how to do it, because you haven't done it.

You need to learn the ability to change.

I want you to imagine now that you're a new starter in your business (if you are, then this will be easy). Imagine that nothing is in place at all: no branding, no marketing, no processes, no clients, no services or products, no pricing.

To give you the best chance with your new future, you've decided to recruit your ideal business coach and mentor. Your new coach is as excited as you are; they're knowledgeable, they're experienced, and they know all about your business sector and your perfect target client. They know the industry, and they love your business with passion, and they really want to help you make it the best business it can be.

I want you to imagine now that this person is you. Be new to your business for this task.

Sometimes, when we start a business, we set it up from a place of lack of knowledge, skills, certainty, money, creativity, or guidance... therefore, it ISN'T the best it can be.

Maybe you even know that you are not doing your best; you are just *carrying on,* as it is easier, even if deep down you believe there is probably a much better way.

We need to bring it to life. I need you to use your imagination for this next task...

TASK:
I want you to stand up and take some deep breaths to feel calm.

Now, allow yourself to imagine a person standing next to you. This imaginary person feels familiar. You automatically feel drawn to them; you trust them and know they are going to help you.

This person next to you, is YOU—a different version of you. It is the very best business version of you... Happy, experienced, successful, knowledgeable, confident, secure, valued—an empowered business owner. You're really doing well, everyone around you is proud, you're in flow, and you're on your A-game. You enjoy serving the most perfect and grateful clients on the planet. This is the version of you that you've strived to be and imagined: the best business version of yourself. You are amazing, aren't you!

I want you to imagine what THIS version of you is thinking about your to-do list: all those things that you're not doing, or all the things that you know need to happen—some of them that are not even on a list. Maybe you know you need a better website with better leads; maybe this version of you *knows* that blogging would work. Really watch this version of yourself viewing your to-do list, and notice their reaction.

You can have a conversation with that version of you too. Ask this best version of yourself what they would do if they were starting again. How would they structure things? Whom would they serve? What would they do with each element that you've previously been stuck with, or that you deep-down *know needs to change* since you launched (the marketing, sales process, and everything else)?

Once you have all the information from the best business version of yourself, I want you to step into that version of YOU. Do it physically, emotionally, and mentally. It is the safest, most natural, and best thing for you to do. Really embrace how they feel to you and how you feel to them, as well as how they stand, what they are thinking, and what they can see so clearly and effortlessly with a bird's-eye view of your business.

How does this NEW version view the world?
How does their self-talk sound in your head?
Whom do they choose to work with?
How creative and sure are you as this amazing business-owning version of yourself?
What do you call yourself as this version?
What does the future look like, now that you are this best business version of yourself?

Do you want to stay as this upgraded version? You can do that, and blend totally.

I hope this was a useful process for you. It's an adapted version of NLP perceptual positions, or *empty chair* in therapy or coaching.

Sometimes you get so close to your business that you can't see the wood for the trees; you don't understand what is needed or what needs to leave. You need a different perspective—a higher perspective—which is the empowered and confident version of yourself. *You are amazing, aren't you!*

Chapter 12

ConfidenceAbility

"Of course, you'll cope; you have a 100% success rate
of coping with past challenge."
~ Vivienne Joy

We all want, need, and admire confidence. Real confidence. Not the bravado often displayed to hide insecurity, which often shows up as arrogance—we spot that shit a mile off and move quickly away from it. It's a natural reaction.

There is no *fake it until you make it* with confidence.

Confidence is attractive, in every sense of the word. Inner confidence shows immediately. The owner wears it well and comfortably, and like they have never been any other way. We are drawn to it. Confidence gives us certainty, and we need certainty in certain aspects of our lives.

What do you think and feel when you see somebody that's got all the confidence?

Do you think that they've got it all going on, and that they seem to be calm and collected, or do you think and wonder why you can't be like that? They don't have a dry mouth, their words come out eloquently, they don't seem to have any physiological symptoms of anxiety or nerves, and they are not shaking—why is that?

Somebody once asked how I overcome nerves. I thought for a moment, and answered, "I don't have any self-talk around nerves, so I'm not nervous."

Nerves are created by self-talk.
No self-talk, no nerves, no insecurity, no anxiety.

Imagine if you approached everything with a sense of knowing; always knowing that what you were going to say and do was ideal, and how you were coming across was absolutely as you wanted it to be. How would it feel?

If confidence is an issue for you, it's your self-talk that is causing confidence sabotage; it's creating your anxiety- like symptoms.

What's the difference between anxiety, stress, and a panic attack?

There are lines crossed that make a big difference to a person's physiology for each of these experiences.

A panic attack is anxiety on another level... *Another level of self-talk*! It is a threatening challenge to survival. The MORE often and severe the self-talk, the more the symptoms occur, and the more self-talk there is. Before you know it, *you're in a self-talk cycle*, and a state of sheer internal panic.

A panic attack should actually be called a "protection attack." Your unconscious primal brain (your reptilian brain) is responding to your fear/debilitating self-talk. It thinks that what you are saying to it is true! It thinks that things are so bad that we are in big shit trouble, and need to act fast. Your unconscious mind then acts as if you are in a state of attack, and brings about all the physiological changes needed to defend or run.

Fight or flight is a natural process, allowing you to stay alive. It is being unnecessarily triggered by your danger self-talk: "I am not good enough; I can't cope; I am too nervous. What if I forget what to say, and what if I get found out?"

Sound familiar?

In days gone by, if you were a caveman or woman, and had a lion chasing you, your body would go into *flight mode*, and an advanced response in your body would happen to make you zoom to safety.

Flight body response is VERY powerful; you are an amazing machine...

- A rush of adrenaline is released to bring blood to muscles, and powerful brain chemicals arrive to get you to be motivated to run fast. In the body, it shows up as that nervous feeling that makes your hands and knees shake, gives you a dry mouth, and makes your face and neck flush. It is preparing you to run like fuck.

- Your breathing changes from deep and slow, to shallow and faster, only serving the vital organs to allow you to take in oxygen more quickly, and to run faster. It also allows you to pant, to recover from your escape.

- Your vision shifts, and you have tunnel vision (rather than peripheral) to allow you to see far away safety, and you would have more focus to run to a safe place. Have you ever felt so scared or nervous that everything seemed to look slightly strange and blurred, like you couldn't see straight?

- Your digestive system speeds up to provide more energy, and your bowel acts to dump whatever it's holding, to allow you to move faster (ever felt sick and needed a nervous toilet stop before a big event?).

All these autonomous responses are designed to give you the support you need when you need to SURVIVE! Your body is very clever, and responds to external and internal influence, which, in the state of anxiety, stress, fear, or panic, is your "Oh shit" self-talk.

So, how can you stop this from happening?

The first thing we *need to do* is stop your anxiety-creating thoughts. The thoughts create the "I can't cope" type self-talk.

Think about the things you say to yourself that create this auto nervous response... "Will they like me?" "What if I fall over?" "What if I get found out?" "What if he's cheating on me?" "What will they think if I'm late?" "What if I can't pay the rent?" "What if I fail?"... Very common panic-inducing self-talk that you might just recognise.

TASK:
Think now about the areas where you are lacking in confidence, be it in relationships, friendships, your job, your career, your business, your family, your body or appearance, your credibility or capability, or anything else.

Grab your pen and write down YOUR *can't cope* fear talk; think about the last time you were nervous, and remember what you said to yourself and what happened.

What you are actually saying with all of this talk is, "What if I can't cope?"

You can, and you will; you always have! Think of your life to date; you have a 100% success rate of survival.

OK, so you may not have thrived in times of adversity, and you may have gained some dodgy coping strategies, but cope you did. You've definitely survived, so give yourself some credit!

So, now that we know you can definitely survive, let's calm that self-talk down! Calm your poor mind and body. They are in a constant state of red alert, in case you need to run. In the business world, we call it *under pressure*, or *stressed*.

Unless you are actually under attack, or at risk of being eaten or killed, then your self-talk should be of calm, coping, and safety. When you're at a networking event, a meeting, or a tricky social occasion, you're not being chased by a lion—well, not in the UK anyway, and certainly not anywhere I've been!

So, if some of that *I can't cope* type self-talk starts, shut it up by saying to yourself, "Thank you for reminding me that I used to believe I couldn't cope, but I cope fabulously, thank you." Sounds too simple, but it really is that simple. Say it repeatedly! Change your self-talk.

Then we need to let the unconscious know that it's all safe and OK, and that we're not on the run...

Take a big, deep breath in. Then, exhale, whilst making that noise of relief that you make when you have conquered something—aaaarrrrrrrrrrrr, that's better—and smile. Do this a few times to turn off your red alert. It is the main physical external sign that you can give to your reptilian brain that everything's OK. If you were running away from a lion, when you got to the other end, you would definitely breathe a BIG SIGH OF RELIEF, and be thankful to be alive. So, by doing this, your unconscious thinks, "Ah, OK, the attack is over. We can go back to our preferred way of running the body." That deep breath and outward verbal sigh allows the adrenaline to leave your body and remove the nervous symptoms.

Then, I want you to say to yourself, or even out loud, "It's all okay; everything is okay. I am safe." You can even look around and check that there's no danger, to reassure yourself (and your unconscious) that you are safe. Say out loud, "I am safe, I am well, I can relax."

Notice your breathing return to normal—vision is corrected, stomach stops churning, hands stop shaking—and breathe.

This is how you start to be the boss of it, and build your confidence. If you're in the fight-or-flight state daily, everything in your world is being restricted. All your blood vessels are being constricted, and you certainly won't be looking for love, connection, or joy—*you are too busy simply surviving!*

You will be more confident in some areas than others!

Exercise is the one thing for me that I am not confident about. I don't have much confidence at all. I'm just not very good at it as I avoided most of it, for most of my life. If someone invites me to go on a long walk, I immediately compare my level of size, age, and fitness to theirs, and I assume it will be too far and too fast for me. I won't be able to keep up, and they will get frustrated with me. I will be thirsty, and what if I need the toilet? (Remember what the fear response does to the bowel!) I find myself making lots of excuses, and ultimately won't go.

Can you hear my self-talk? Ridiculous, eh, and probably not true! The more I tell myself that I'm not good at exercise, the more I have to rev myself up, even for a short walk. It's exhausting. My self-talk creates some of the symptoms that other people would experience in *their* times of no business confidence—public speaking being the most common. I don't get those symptoms when I'm public speaking because I have all the confidence on the planet where that's concerned... Instead, I get that whole *oh, I just need the loo, dry mouthed, heightened breathing* feeling about going for a non-purposeful walk. To make it happen, I change my self-talk, take a bottle of water, and keep my breathing in check, and then I'm fine. Oddly, it doesn't happen if I am walking for a purpose, such as shopping, etc. *I have rules around when to be nervous or anxious. This is common.*

What are your rules around when to be anxious?

It won't be everything in your life; there'll be some things you're really confident with and won't experience any of these symptoms.

TASK:
Grab your pen and write down the self-talk you have around the things you're not confident with. Be totally honest, and put as many into words as you can.

Now do the same with those things you're confident with and good at. You may notice that there isn't much self-talk involved in the positive; you just get on with it.

It's important to know your *strategy for being confident*, because then we can map it over to the things you are not so confident with.

I can tell you that one of them will be very empowering self-talk (creating calm confidence), with all the "oh, you're good at this;" "I'm looking forward to it;" "oh, this will be great;" "won't it be an amazing outcome when everybody will think I'm amazing;" "I'll feel amazing;" "I'm excited," versus the negative self-talk (creating high anxiety) of "I don't know what I'm saying;" "I don't know what I'm doing;" "who am I to think?" "Who am I to speak or even breathe?"

The next time you're in a networking event, and it's coming around to you for your *stand up and stand out with your pitch,* take note of what you're saying to yourself, and how it is making your body react. Change your self-talk to support yourself; or better still, *think nothing*. If you're not saying anything to yourself, you won't have any of the physiological conditions of nerves, and you won't have that dry mouth and forget your words. *You will be calm and confident.*

Without a *can't cope* belief, there's no self-talk. If you believed you were good at everything, your self-talk would be focused around being very good at everything, and you'd enjoy it.

Remember where the negative self-talk comes from? *Your schemas.* Those that are disempowering you and running your self-talk, running you down to the ground, and having you running for the hills in times of pressure. You need to get rid of those scheming little terrors, and then none of the symptoms will even be there!

You need to understand where that schema, belief, trigger, anchor comes from; because, very often, whatever you're thinking isn't the truth; it really isn't true at all. Wouldn't it be lovely to be able to have that same amazing feeling of confidence, in **ALL your life,** that you have in the area that you know you're confident in?

If you're not confident in relationships, it's probably because, somewhere, somebody has told you you're not good enough. If you're not good in your business, it will be because, somewhere, you probably know you should be doing something better or differently, or maybe you're still quite unsure of where you sit in that marketplace, or just don't have the skills and feel out of your depth.

Visit www.MindsetForBusiness.co.uk to learn how you can afford yourself the support to get out of your own way with mindset coaching, plus learn from me the business skills to make a strong business foundation.

TASK:
Let's work out for you where that schema comes from for each thing you would like to be more confident with.

It may be something to do with school, or much younger. I would suggest that if you find something that's between five and 10, then you've probably hit the belief that stopped you from doing this *thing* confidently.

From your earlier task, go and write down when, where, and how you learnt to NOT be confident. Your unconscious will show you a picture, or a feeling, if you ask it nicely. Notice what you hear, see, and feel during this process.

Then, as in previous chapters, ask if that schema was ever true, and if it is true now. Then decide what you would like to believe and say to yourself instead (new enabling self-talk).

Check in with your unconscious to make sure it agrees with your new belief. You will be surprised at how differently you can feel.

I hope that this is making sense for you; you need to be sure. Confidence is an inside job—it comes from within. If you don't feel confident in everything you're saying, thinking, feeling, and doing, then the whole world will notice, and that's where you start to feel more edgy. *It's a self-fulfilling prophecy.*

Take some time to understand where your beliefs come from around whatever it is you're not confident with, and then make sure you shift it with this process.

Next time you're feeling like you're in a position where you're not sure what to do, look around and say, "I'm safe, I'm not under attack, and there is no threat to me," and breathe deeply and smile. There are no tigers chasing you, just your own imagination.

Chapter 13

PalpAbility

"Nothing is more important than reconnecting with your bliss. Nothing is as rich. Nothing is more real."
~ Deepak Chopra

Palpitations... Your heart beating fast, blood rushing through your veins, endorphins tingling your skin, and endorphins bringing a warm glow from the inside out. It's the joy and happiness you feel when totally connected and alive.

Can you remember the last time you felt this?

Which things get you excited, driven, and motivated? Take a moment to remember. It's the high vibe visible energy that gets your clients and prospects excited to be working with you, to say yes to you, to pay you, to have the outcomes they need.

What is PalpAbility?

There's a fine line between excitement and fear. Sometimes we get the two mixed up!

I want you to think about a time where you were in a heightened emotional state. It could have been anger, excitement, sadness, or fear—these are the 4 main emotional states we focus on, as they tend to over-arch everything we experience. Think about situations and events, like getting married, getting fired, or informed of a bereavement; jumping out of a plane, driving a race car, or any adrenalin-fuelled experience. As I've mentioned a few times throughout this book, public speaking seems to be the one that gets the palpitations going for most people. In fact, people would reportedly rather die than get up in front of a bunch of people and do a talk!

A bit like anxiety, there are a host of noticeable, physiological conditions that go with palpability: dry mouth, slightly blurred vision, maybe going red in the face, fast breathing—all the things that get your heart racing, and you know that you're truly alive, be it through fear or through excitement. Do you see, they are very similar! Your unconscious mind doesn't know the difference between:

- Real danger
- Feared danger
- CREATED danger (excitement)

Next time you think you're nervous or anxious, check in with yourself to see if you are in fact, EXCITED! *There is a fine line.*

If your life doesn't have palpability, your day to day will be the same, routine, expected, and safe experience. *Which sounds nice and easy, doesn't it?* Unfortunately, the basic human need for certainty, to be **safe and stay the same,** is annoyingly challenged by another human need for uncertainty—**excitement and new experiences.**

If we are not having them, we feel like we are just surviving and not thriving. *Sound familiar?*

Too much safety and not enough palpability will be unexciting, and even boring! There'll be nothing making your heart race; nothing making you want to jump out of bed like you did as a kid on Christmas morning. Nothing making you want to drive yourself to success. No inner challenges or feelings of pride like you had when you passed exams or your driving test! No buzz, no un-certainty, no pulse... Just graft and daily life. Zzzzzzzzz—I nearly fell asleep typing it!

It's quite common for entrepreneurs to want the buzz! *By nature, they want more, and are bigger risk takers. Let's face it; not knowing where your next mortgage payment is coming from is palpable each month*! If we didn't want the rewards, we wouldn't take the risk. We'd stay safe in jobs with pensions and holiday pay. (I vaguely remember those days!)

If this is you, and you crave adventure and excitement, palpability is essential. If you haven't got it, you NEED to get it, or you will often wonder, "What is the fucking point of being alive!"

TASK:
I want you to remember a time when you felt excited—REALLY, really excited. It could've been because of anything— getting on a plane for the first time (I'm typing this whilst at the airport), having your first date, first kiss, first (ahem) time having sex, cooking your first Christmas dinner, opening a gift that you knew was special, proposing to somebody, or getting a new gadget—whatever it is that got you VERY excited.

***Close your eyes and recall that clearly now in your mind.* See what you saw then through your eyes, as if you were fully reliving it. Hear what you heard then, feel what you felt, and notice all the small details as you feel your body respond to this powerful and exciting memory. If you're doing this fully and effectively, after a few minutes, you'll recall the FULL physiological conditioning of that memory, and it will feel amazing.**

Powerful, eh? I know you can feel it.

The power of your unconscious mind is literally mind blowing. You're experiencing this in all wonder and joy right now. This process is what we call in NLP, a *state change*. You have changed your physiological, mental, and emotional state with a simple thought, wish, or memory. *(Remember, your unconscious doesn't know the difference between make believe and real memories.)*

You are state changing all day long and don't even realise it.

Other people are inadvertently changing your state too (social media, traffic, phone calls, etc.)!

Have you ever been having a perfectly lovely day, and then you see a post on social media and feel sad or angry? When you truly realise this social impact, you'll guard what you let into your mind. I no longer read newspapers or watch the news channels. I'm selective over what appears in my social feeds. I only watch certain things on TV (no murders or miserable stuff, as it literally darkens my mood). Have you ever watched a horror film and been scared to go to bed with the light off? *(Remember, the unconscious doesn't know the difference between your real life fact and soap operas!)*

I strongly suggest that you *guard your waking thoughts* and experiences, like your life and mental health depended on it. Let only the positive and true thoughts through, to keep your beautiful state for as much of your day as you possibly can.

If you feel it slip (and it will, it's life), you can choose to change your state back to happy and calm, just like this task at any time. If you wake up in the morning thinking, "Oh no, I've got another day of admin work," "got to speak to that client," or "got that problem to solve," You will start your day in a *bad state,* and it won't take much to worsen it. Not a very powerful and supportive way to talk to yourself about your business and another day you've been granted life, is it! In fact, your self-talk sounds rather depressing, stressing, and repressing. *Stop starting your day in a shit state!*

The word, *depressed*, gets banded about way too easily and too often in my opinion. Real depression is a chemical imbalance. Many people are prescribed anti-depressant drugs and often have what I call *circumstantial depression*: an emotional state brought on by trauma or an event in time where coping didn't go too well. It's simple to track this back to divorce, loss, redundancy, etc. If you're thinking and telling yourself negative and bullying things on a continual basis (daily, hourly, or all day), you are making yourself feel worse, and miserable.

Unsupported, even by yourself; being your own aggressor, bully, or repressor—you certainly won't be living a palpable and joyful life. *If this is you, what could you think instead when you wake up, to empower yourself?*

What makes you feel like your heart starts to race a bit? Boredom and certainty can't live where there is a heart racing, and you'll soon be alert and ready to have a fab day! Remember what you said made you excited, at the beginning of this chapter. Maybe it was the excitement of hitting that target, helping that client, finding a new client, or creating a video that's going to change the destination of your business. *Go and get excited for life!*

What can you think to start your day in the best way? Many people practice an *attitude of gratitude*. It's hard to be sulky and bored when you are meditating or concentrating on thinking about all the things you are lucky to have! Feel and experience the people in your life, your home, your car, your passion for life, your skills, your hair... anything that you are truly grateful to have!

Maybe you are thinking that you are not capable of thinking of exciting things for your business right now, and maybe life feels a bit shit. Sometimes we get into a bit of a funk, where we're wading through treacle. It normally means that there's something not right with what we're doing or what we're thinking; those two things will create how we're feeling.

If you're in this mindset of the blues, ask yourself, "What is the treacle I'm wading through; why can't I just take my feet out of the treacle and step somewhere else?" As you step out of the treacle, look back at it to get a different perspective, and understand what's creating impalpability. Once you realise and release this, you can work out how to inject some palpability into your day, week, month, and life.

Maybe you can even remove the bits that are making the treacle so sticky.

Maybe some guru said that you need to get up at five o'clock every morning to be successful! This will be a struggle if your body clock prefers half seven. Listen to your body, always. IT is getting signals from your unconscious on how to fix things, and you just need to learn how to listen and act.

Maybe you're trying to work at 10 o'clock at night, whereas actually you know you're no good in the evening. How you structure your day is very important when you're your own boss. When are your peak performance times and those that are more functional? Schedule accordingly.

If you are trying to do admin when you are naturally at your most creative, you will feel shut down and disengaged.

Get to know your entrepreneurial, business-owning self—you are different from who you were in a job.

I'm not good at anything creative or expansive, such as design or copywriting, in the afternoon. I'm pretty much useless, in fact—so, guess when I am at my best as a coach? Yes, in the afternoon. It's when I hold sessions. I'm joyfully sitting and listening, observing, understanding, nurturing and caring, because that is the space that I'm more comfortable in at that time of day. I'm absolutely the most creative about midnight—11pm to 1am—I'm in my best business self-power, with no interruptions or distractions, and nobody needs me apart from my *life purpose*. If I want to do functional things and be the doer in my business (like the worker bee), this happens first thing in the morning, anywhere from 5am to 10am. When you notice your regular patterns, you can schedule your day accordingly.

TASK:
Understand how your heart races and beats, how your energy flows, and how your mental rhythms work for you, and understand how to make your day feel great and in tune with you.

Grab your paper and draw out your typical day, in days and hours, on a columned grid. Then work out when you are best suited to doing which things, and create yourself a default diary so that you get everything done *in tune* with yourself...

- **Functional – admin and processes**
- **Creative – marketing, design, and promotions**
- **Connected – sales and social posts, meetings/networking**
- **Energised – delivering your service**
- **Calm – blog writing and positioning pieces**
- **Tired – STOP and enjoy doing something else**

If your day doesn't feel nice, then you're not going to do the necessary things, and you'll feel a failure or overwhelmed and stressed. You need to get the adrenaline pumping at the right times, because if you're not excited about what you can do to help people, then they're not going to be excited either, and no one wants to deal with somebody who looks bored in their business!

Have you ever been to a networking meeting, or seen posts or videos where it's absolutely clear that the business owner loves what they do and are passionate and driven—and then notice the exact opposite in someone else, where they're not remotely excited to get up in the morning, and they lack lustre! *Do you want to do business with them?*

We want to deal with people that are excited, on top of their game, buzzing, and really into what they're doing. If you're not into what you're doing, then find someone to help you, because maybe you're doing the wrong thing, or doing the right thing in the wrong way, or at the wrong time of day. As always, I'm happy to help.

Look for clues outside of work... Think about the things that get you excited outside of your business—walking the dog, cooking, crafting, or anything that gets you into that space where you feel great—and work out how you can bring those into different parts of your day to create *good feelings and palpability*... that energy will then transcend into your business, bringing it to life.

I love being on the stage, I love public speaking, I love being the centre of attention, and I have ever since I was little. *So, what did I do to bring that palpability and excitement into my business life?* I decided to set up big events where I'm in control of success or failure (full adrenalin rush). I'm at the centre of it all, everyone has an amazing time, and it absolutely fills me up. It also exhausts me to be in that high adrenaline state for a long time, so I have to plan a recovery, as my body just says, eventually, "Whoa, let's have a little chill now; just calm down a minute there, little Miss Empowerment!" It's a bit like running a marathon: At the end of it, you are wiped out, but blissfully happy, proud, victorious, and filled with endorphins and satisfaction.

Balance certainty and uncertainty correctly in your world; otherwise, you will experience boredom or burnout, and either way, you'll be no good to anyone! *What is your right balance?*

As we leave this chapter, think how you get your passion served. What is driving you every day? What is the one thing that ALWAYS gets you buzzing, that you absolutely love? It could be getting positive responses on a social post. It could be somebody telling you how amazing you are (you can see recognition is high up on my value set). It could be genuinely just seeing somebody really enjoying using your service. It could be getting your spreadsheets and expenses in order. It could be knowing your numbers. It could be a fully automated process that delivers revenue. It could be a whole day off each week! Whatever it is, make sure you have that for yourself and your business *every day*—you're worth it!

If your heart's beating fast and you're excited each day, your prospects and clients will be too, and that is a great place to be, I promise.

Chapter 14

AccountAbility

"You must take personal responsibility. You cannot change the circumstances, the seasons, or the wind, but you can change yourself. That is something you have charge of."
~ Jim Rohn

Are you accountable?

For yourself, your business, or your family?

Are you accountable to anyone? *Who is your boss?*

We need to be accountable to get things done. When I run coaching, training, and mentoring sessions, accountability is always the one thing everybody wants and KNOWS they need! They want an ass kicking, or to be prodded, reminded, or lovingly nurtured, depending on the procrastinated task.

Do you need someone to tell you what to do, how to do it, when to do it, and to make sure you've done it?

This micro-managing NEED is a childlike behaviour pattern. Children mainly need to be taught and told to tidy their room; how to do it, when to do it, and bribed to do it! I'm sure those of you that have children will understand.

That isn't the way that adults should work, really. Adults should have a different way of thinking and feeling about things; they should want to feel that they've achieved something—it's in our blood from our hunting evolution—we love achievement, it releases a chemical rush to our brain, and we feel significant and valued. *Powerful stuff.*

Accountability could be called achievability.

My first question to you is, "Do you procrastinate?" *Do you?* Let's be honest about this. You can call it whatever you like: needing to relax, giving yourself care, didn't have time, there were more important things. These are all beautiful little ways of saying that you're intentionally procrastinating. There are also ways of saying it that would be more honest—a bit like my CV/resume at the beginning of the book! "It wasn't important enough;" "I don't know the value of completion;" "Nobody will know or care if I don't do it;" 'I'm not really sure how to do it." If you consistently don't do things, it means that it's just not that important to you, and if it's not that important, then you won't do it. It's as simple as that, really.

When did you last procrastinate? Think about the last time you procrastinated. It may have been today. (I'm grinning, as I procrastinated for 3 days writing this chapter, to be ironic; my desk is soooooooo tidy now though!)

What are you putting off? It may be that you're reading this and procrastinating, or trying to find ways to stop procrastinating! Will the thing you are putting off make you more money, make you feel better, give you more freedom or peace of mind?

I coached a guy, named Mark, who was procrastinating about his website for a year. A whole year, and when we started to look at the reasons, it was clear: He didn't realise the value of that website to his business. He didn't understand what he could be doing with his business: driving traffic, building an audience, selling things, and capturing data and contact details. After an hour of DREAMING of what the capability of his website COULD be, finishing his website became his only goal for that month! Mission accomplished.

Accountability is all about solving procrastination.

If you want to achieve something, work out the true value of it. If you're still not doing it, then you've got another reason running, a fear schema, or lack of skills. *It always boils down to these things.*

TASK:
Write a list of what you are procrastinating about. You might even just be transferring your to-do list on to a fresh sheet of paper at this point! It could be anything in life or business—creating videos, cleaning your house, tidying up your office, following up a quote, passing your driving test, leaving your partner—anything big or small that you're procrastinating about. List the lot—it's like a procrastination amnesty!

Then, take one at a time, and answer the 4 questions for each.

- **What is the perceived value of completing the task?**
- **What is the REAL value of completing the task? Understanding this should be enough to bump it up the list. *Imagine the possibilities.***
- **What skills or resources do you need to start, do, and complete? Can you get them?**
- **What would be the benefit of NOT completing the task (remember secondary gain)?**

Have you discovered what's truly stopping you? *(I'll give you a clue: it's never lack of time!)*

What is getting in your way? What's keeping you stuck? There will be something. It could be that you don't have the skills to do it; in which case, find some training, find someone to teach you, or outsource it.

It could be that you genuinely don't have the time to do it (coughs). Writing this book took loads of time—time very well spent! I had loads of excuses not to finish. "Oh, I'm sorry, Book Architect, I didn't create that piece of self-coaching for my clients to enjoy, because I just didn't have the time." "I was too busy coaching one to one, to write my book!" "I wanted to make sure it was up-to-date…" You can understand how these were valid excuses. Had I known the power and impact of this book, it would have been my NUMBER ONE PRIORITY!

How you choose to spend your time and life will shape your joy and success. Choose wisely my friend. Spend the time on the things that are most valuable.

Most people don't like doing parts of their business; it's normally the expenses, the invoicing, and chasing money. Sometimes it's following up sales leads. Either they love housework or hate it; there's always something in your life you don't want to do. For me, it was ironing. I don't do ironing. I totally removed it from my life. If I need anything ironed, someone else does it for me. It used to drive me insane.

I could have said to somebody, "Please make me accountable for doing my ironing," but I handled it differently. When I looked at where the belief came from, I remembered that my mum hated ironing. I can remember her standing there with the iron, saying, "I bloody hate ironing all Sunday night, ironing your father's shirts." I can hear her now, and I used to agree with her and think, "What a waste of time. He's just going to wear them and crease them, and you're going to wash them, and you have to iron them again—what a waste of bloody time." My belief and resistance comes from my mother.

Where do yours come from?

Lots of people struggle with accountability because if they do all they should do to be successful, they'll earn all the money they want.

Money beliefs run many schemas! Do you believe you can earn and deserve lots of money? Should you be charging more for your thing? Do you feel guilty for asking for money, or for sending the invoice?

Do the belief change work in this book, and get out of your own way with that. It will be the biggest gift you can give yourself. In fact, I run a free, 7 Day Intensive Money Mindset Reset, once a year, to help people shift. Visit the website to book on to the next one!

You need to understand where your beliefs come from and what's keeping you stuck. Crap money beliefs will absolutely wreck your potential and business—they'll wreck your life, actually! Take it from me, my parents were both compulsive gamblers, and I'm a reformed compulsive gambler, so I know more about money mindset than most!

The adrenaline that we talked about in the palpability chapter can also be caused by that fear of doing something, **fear of getting out of your own way**. It may be that you're getting your palpability by staying fearful and stuck.

If you have a massive to-do list (and I see some crackers, as you can imagine), you will be in a slightly high adrenaline state most of the time, with an "I've got lots to do," and an "I'm so busy" energy. You may be living there every day… *Let's check!*

TASK:
I want you to imagine now whatever is on your list (because this is all about the list; let's be honest).

Now imagine that list doesn't exist. In your mind's eye, screw it up and put it somewhere. None of that list exists. All you need to focus on are the things that are TRULY important.

Now make a NEW LIST. Make a new list with just 10 things, and see how much calmer and easier that feels.

I can tell you, it'll feel very different—a new, achievable, and exciting list.

Most of the stuff on that old list is you procrastinating about old things you thought you had to do—stuff you probably thought you should have done, were told you should do, maybe three months ago, three years ago, or even longer for some people... *and they are definitely no longer relevant*! If those tasks had been relevant, you would have done them already, wouldn't you?

Focus on your top 10 *GET DONE PRIORITIES.*

I have a client who said, "Vivienne, can you please remind me that I need to do that task by next Wednesday?" I said, "You don't need me for that; set an alarm on your phone!" We have smart phones; be smart and use them. Set an alarm, and that will remind you. You don't need accountability for that.

What you may need is somebody to help you understand what is stopping you from achieving the things you say that you want to achieve, what triggers your fears, and where they come from...

I want you to think of a time now where you **didn't procrastinate about something,** because there will be lots of times when you haven't procrastinated, when you had an idea or you made a decision and TOOK immediate, empowered, intelligent Action.

The decision itself can BE the procrastination.

I have a friend who's trying to decide whether to leave her partner or not, and she hasn't decided. It's a very painful process for her. The decision is painful, like a real head fuck. The actual action after the decision can be tricky; but it is more about achieving the decision (doing, not feeling). *The decision is the painful part.*

What are you deciding right now about your list? Your business? Yourself? Me? Life?

Decide the possible actions, and list them. Choose the best one. Do it. Take the action, and achieve it without any procrastination—no accountability coaching needed—just beautiful flow, and you felt the result of it.

What will you do next?

What is your best business self REALLY capable of?

Enjoy the journey of finding out… Best of luck, my friend. If I can help, look me up.